Foundations of IT Security

Other publications by Van Haren Publishing

Van Haren Publishing (VHP) specializes in titles on Best Practices, methods and standards within four domains:
- IT management
- Architecture (Enterprise and IT)
- Business management and
- Project management

VHP is also publisher on behalf of leading companies and institutions:
The Open Group, IPMA-NL, PMI-NL, CA, Getronics, Quint, ITSqc, LLC, The Sox Institute and ASL BiSL Foundation

Topics are (per domain):

IT (Service) Management / IT Governance
ASL
BiSL
CATS
CMMI
CoBiT
ISO 17799
ISO 27001
ISO 27002
ISO/IEC 20000
ISPL
IT Service CMM
ITIL® V2
ITIL® V3
ITSM
MOF
MSF
ABC of ICT

Architecture (Enterprise and IT)
Archimate®
GEA®
TOGAF™

Business Management
EFQM
ISA-95
ISO 9000
ISO 9001:2000
SixSigma
SOX
SqEME®
eSCM

Project/Programme/ Risk Management
A4-Projectmanagement
ICB / NCB
MINCE®
M_o_R®
MSP™
PMBOK® Guide
PRINCE2™

For the latest information on VHP publications, visit our website: www.vanharen.net.

Foundations
of IT Security
Based on ISO27001/27002

Jule Hintzbergen

Kees Hintzbergen

André Smulders

Hans Baars

Van Haren
PUBLISHING

Colophon

Title:	Foundations of IT Security
Subtitle:	Based on ISO27001/27002
Series:	Best Practice
Authors:	Jule Hintzbergen, Kees Hintzbergen, André Smulders, Hans Baars
Editor:	Steve Newton
Reviewers:	- Norman Crocker (Cronos Consulting) - Steven Doan (Schlumberger, USA) - James McGovern (The Hartford) - Prof. Pauline C. Reich (Waseda University School of Law) - Bernard Roussely (Cyberens Technologies & Services) - Tarot Wake (Invictus Security)
Publisher:	Van Haren Publishing, Zaltbommel, www.vanharen.net
ISBN:	978 90 8753 568 1
Print:	Second edition, first impression, May 2010
Design and Layout:	CO2 Premedia, Amersfoort-NL
Copyright:	© Van Haren Publishing, 2010, excluded appendix B
Printer:	Wilco, Amersfoort-NL

For any further inquiries about Van Haren Publishing, please send an email to: info@vanharen.net

Preface

The word 'security' has by its nature a negative feel to it. Security is, after all, only applied when there is reason to: when there is a risk that things will not go as they should. In this book various topics about IT security are mentioned, as simply as possible because IT security is everyone's responsibility, although many users of IT systems don't realize this.

Security is not new, and indeed the roots for IT security can be found centuries ago when, for example, the Egyptians used non-standard hieroglyphs carved into monuments and the Romans invented the so called ceasar cypher to encrypt messages. In addition, physical security is very old, think about old fortresses and defenses like the Great Wall of China. In recent years physical security is more and more dependent upon IT and physical security is also necessary to protect information, so there IT comes together again.

This book started originally two years ago in Dutch and then there couldn't be found a way to get it to you out there. The book was adapted by EXIN as study book and it is also suitable for anyone who would like to know more about IT security, since you can use it as awareness document for IT security. The first translation to English never made it, and needed a lot of rework. This book is intended to be read by everyone who wants to know more about IT security but also for people that want to have a basic understanding about IT security as a foundation to learn more.

What do you find in this book?
At first there are basic understanding and address common topics such as the fundamental principles of security and information security, and risk management. From there the book goes on to look at the architecture, processes and information that are needed for a basic understanding of what IT security is about. We then go deeper in threats and risks together with risk management.

Business assets are then discussed, what are they and how should they be used and maintained? Later chapters are about the measures that can be taken to protect IT assets. Firstly we mention physical measures, that's were it all starts, the door to go into a building. Secondly we mention the technical measures, including encryption. Thirdly we mention the organizational measures. Organizational security measures are often inextricably linked with technical measures. Where relevant, we will refer to the technical measures that are necessary in order to be able to carry out or enforce these organizational measures.

Finally we write about managing the communication and operating procedures that are necessary for the effective management and control of the IT within an organization.

We also include some information about law and regulations. This is an international book and we cannot put everything in there. To find more about local laws we suggest you look on the Internet.

This book is recommended as a study book for the Information Security Foundation based on ISO/IEC 27002 exams of EXIN.

EXIN is an independent, international examination institute for IT professionals. EXIN's mission is to improve the quality of the IT sector as well as that of IT professionals. In order to achieve these goals, EXIN develops exam requirements and IT exams. EXIN provides four examinations in Information Security. These examinations are based on ISO/IEC 27002. You can take exams at Foundation, Advanced and Expert level. At the Expert level you are tested not only on your knowledge of ISO/IEC 27002 but also that of ISO/IEC 27001.

The organisation for Information Security Professionals in The Netherlands (PvIB) endorse this book as a very good start in the world of information security. It is a must read.

Fred van Noord, chairman PvIB (Platform voor Informatiebeveiliging)
www.pvib.nl

Acknowledgements

This book has been written from the viewpoint that a basic understanding about IT security is important for everyone. We have tried to put a lot of information in this book without going into too much detail. Besides that, we are all Dutch guys and we were not able to write this book without the help of the reviewers who helped us to improve it.

We would like to thank the reviewers who provided us with valuable comments on the texts we had written. In alphabetical order they are:

Norman Crocker, Cronos Consulting, Silves, Portugal
Steven Doan, Schlumberger, Houston, Texas, USA
James McGovern, The Hartford, Hartford, Connecticut, United States
Prof. Pauline C. Reich, Waseda University School of Law, Tokyo, Japan
Bernard Roussely, Director, Cyberens Technologies & Services, Bordeaux, France
Tarot Wake, Invictus Security, Flintshire, United Kingdom

Content

1. Introduction

This book is intended for everyone in an organization who wishes to have a basic understanding of information security. Knowledge about information security is important to all employees. It makes no difference if you work in a profit- or non-profit organization because the risks that organizations face are equal for all organizations.

Employees need to know why they have to adhere to security rules on a day-to-day basis. Line managers need to have this understanding as they are responsible for the security of information in their department. This basic knowledge is also important for all business people, including those self-employed without employees, as they are responsible for protecting their own information. A certain degree of knowledge is also necessary at home. And of course, this knowledge forms a good basis for those who may be considering a career as an information security specialist, whether as an IT professional or a process manager.

Everyone is involved in information security, often via security countermeasures. These countermeasures are sometimes enforced by regulatory rules and sometimes they are implemented by means of internal rules. Consider, for example, the use of a password on a computer. We often experience measures as a nuisance as these can take up our time and we do not always know what measures they are protecting us against.

The trick to information security is finding the right balance between a number of aspects:
- The quality[1] requirements an organization may have for its information;
- The risks associated with these quality requirements;
- The countermeasures that are necessary to mitigate these risks;
- Ensuring business continuity in the event of a disaster.
- When and whether to report incidents outside the organization.

What is quality?
First you have to decide what you think quality is. At its simplest level, quality answers two questions: 'What is wanted?' and 'How do we do it?' Accordingly, quality's stomping ground has always been the area of processes. From ISO 9000, to the heady heights of Total Quality Management (TQM), quality professionals specify, measure, improve and re-engineer processes to ensure that people get what they want.

So where are we now?
There are as many definitions of quality as there are quality consultants, but commonly accepted variations include:
- 'Conformance to requirements' – Crosby;
- 'Fitness for use' – Juran;
- 'The totality of characteristics of an entity that bear on its ability to satisfy stated and implied need' - ISO 8402:1994;

---

1   http://syque.com/articles/what_is_quality/what_is_quality_1.htm

- Quality models for business, including the Deming Prize, the EFQM excellence model and the Baldrige award.

The primary objective of this book is to achieve awareness by students who want to apply for a basic security examination. This book is based on the international ISO 27002 Code of Practice for this information security standard.

This book is also a source of information for the lecturer who wants to question information security students about their knowledge. Each chapter ends with a case study. In order to help with the understanding and coherence of each subject, these case studies include questions relating to the areas covered in the relevant chapters. Examples of recent events that illustrate the vulnerability of information are also included.

The case study starts at a very basic level and grows during the chapters of the book. The starting point is a small bookstore with few employees and few risks. During the chapters this business grows and grows and, at the end, it is a large firm with 120 bookstores and a large web shop. The business risks faced by this bookshop are a thread through this book.

This book is intended to explain the differences between risks and vulnerabilities and to identify how countermeasures can help to mitigate most risks.Due to its general character, this book is also suitable for awareness training or as a reference book in an awareness campaign.

This book is primarily aimed at profit and non-profit organizations, but the subjects covered are also applicable to the daily home environment as well to companies that do not have dedicated information security personnel. In those situations the various information security activities would be carried out by a single person.

After reading the book you will have a general understanding of the subjects that encompass information security. You will also know why these subjects are important and will gain an appreciation of the most common concepts of information security.

2 Case study: Springbooks – an international bookstore

2.1 Introduction

To understand the theory in this book, it will be helpful to translate it to a practical situation. In most situations the reader gets a better understanding of the theory when it is illustrated by a practical case study. In this case study, used throughout all chapters of this book, questions are included that relate to lessons learned in each chapter.

Figure 2.1 Springbooks London Headquarters

This chapter gives an explanatory introduction to the case study. The establishment of the bookstore, the history and the years of growing into an international company are all described.

Springbooks was founded in 1901. During its expansion into an international organization operating within Europe the company has to change and to adjust to its environment. A major part of this is the huge change over the last 50 years in supplying information. As one might imagine there is a big difference in process control between the time Springbooks was founded in 1901, during the emergence of Information and Communication Techniques (ICT) during the 1960s and 1970s through to the ever increasing dependence on ICT nowadays. ICT has become one of the most important tools for Springbooks.

2.2 Springbooks

Springbooks Ltd. is a European operating bookstore. SB is an organization with 120 bookshops, most of which are run on a franchise basis. In total, 50 of the shops are owned by SB itself.

Figure 2.2 Organizational Chart Springbooks in 1901

The first SB was founded in 1901 in Bedrock-on-Thames, UK. Henry Spring opened a bookstore in 1901in a small shop.

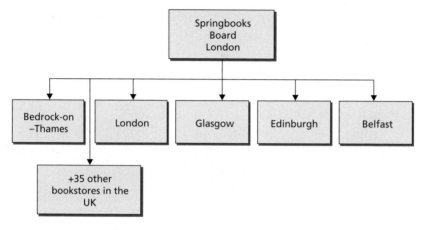

Figure 2.3 Organization of Springbooks 1938

Over time 36 shops were established in all major cities in the UK. Immediately after the end of World War II SB established bookshops in Amsterdam, Copenhagen, Stockholm, Bonn, Berlin and Paris.

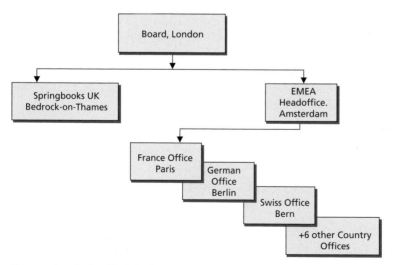

Figure 2.4 Organization of Springbooks 1960

Nowadays SB has shops in all major cities in the EU. The Board of Directors is based at offices in London. European headquarters are in Amsterdam and every country has a central office. All bookstores are accountable to their national office. The national office is accountable to the European Headquarters in Amsterdam. The European headquarters are ultimately accountable to the Board of Directors in London.

In 2000 plans are made to expand the international business into the USA, Canada, Australia and New Zealand by the end of the first decade of 2000. However, because of the banking crisis which arises at the end of 2008, these plans are not carried out, at this moment.

The banking crisis has had a serious affect upon the worth of SB shares. The fact is that one of the first things people economize on are books, newspapers and magazines. All these are core businesses of SB. This resulted in a temporary halt on the plans to expand the overseas market. Investment plans in new stores are frozen and a search for new markets has resulted in new plans.

The board of directors has adopted an old fashioned approach to business for a long time. The Internet was not their way of doing business.

However, an independent consultancy group has advised that SB should launch an online store and not limit sales to simply books, and magazines, but instead look to expand into travel in combination with travel books and, in the longer term, also offer consumer electronics and other consumer goods.

Organization:
London UK:
In the London Headquarters resides the Board of Directors and the overall Chief Information Officer (CIO), Chief Financial Officer (CFO), Chief Procurement Officer (CPO) and Chief Executive Officer (CEO).

Each country has a central office which is responsible for the business in that specific country. The Country Director is responsible to the Unit Director for their particular region.

Bedrock-on-Thames UK:
UK Director (UK is not EU) responsible for the UK bookstores. There is also an UK-CIO, CEO, CFO and a Local Information Security Officer (LISO).

Amsterdam, the Netherlands:
1 EU director (EU without UK)

EU CIO, CEO, CFO, CPO, LISO and the Corporate Information Security Officer (CISO). Springbooks has a partly centralized information security organization. The main way of performing (or handling) information security is directed out of the London headquarters. ISO 27001 and ISO 27002 are the standards to be used in all countries.

In London, there is a Corporate Information Security Manager who has overall responsibility for organizing information security in the corporation. He ensures that information security is part of the daily job of all Springbooks employees.

It is up to the local offices to ensure compliance with local law and regulations. This decentralized part of information security can have an impact on the way information security has to be organized locally.

The national Local Information Security Officer (LISO) is responsible for adherence to both the central rules, and the national rules. He is also responsible for the physical security of the bookstores and Health Safety and Environment of the bookstore employees. In the UK next to the CISM, the LISO is responsible for the information security at the UK bookstores.

Every bookstore has an information security focal point. This is an employee who is accountable for information security in the store and the contact point to the 'national' LISO.

IT is centrally organized. There is a wide area network (WAN) that all stores are connected to. The Springbooks wide area network (WAN) is a computer network that covers a broad area. This is in contrast with local area networks (LANs) in the bookstores that are limited to a single building.

The cash desks are connected to this WAN. Every book that is sold is scanned at the cash desk and registered in a central database. This makes it possible to have an accurate overview of books in stock every (part of the) day. By updating stocks based on sales, Springbooks can ensure that the popular books are always in stock. The speed of restocking depends on the popularity of the book, of course.

Every employee has their own ID that is used to login to the cash desk system. Every book sold, is connected to the employee who produced the invoice. In the same database there is a lot of customer information stored, such as names, addresses and credit card information.

All customer-related information stored in the Springbooks' IT environment makes information security and compliance to (national) privacy laws very important. Unexpected and unauthorized disclosure of the customer database can have huge consequences for the trustworthiness of Springbooks.

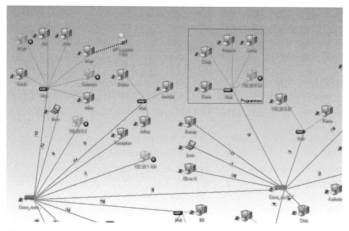

Figure 2.5 Data connections between bookstores are speeding up

3. Definitions

This chapter contains definitions of key concepts in the book. In Appendix A you will find an extensive glossary.

Asset
Anything that has value to the organization.
[ISO/IEC 13335-1:2004]

Availability
Availability ensures the reliable and timely access to data or computing resources by the appropriate personnel. In other words, availability guarantees that the systems are up and running when needed. In addition this concept guarantees that the security services that the security practitioner requires are in working order. [2]

Confidentiality
The concept of confidentiality attempts to prevent the intentional or unintentional disclosure of a message's content. Loss of confidentiality can occur in many ways, such as through the intentional release of private company information or through a misapplication in network rights.

Control
A means of managing risk, including policies, procedures, guidelines, practices or organizational structures, which can be of an administrative, technical, management, or legal nature.
NOTE Control is also used as a synonym for safeguard or countermeasure.

Exposure
An exposure is an instance of being exposed to losses from a threat agent.

Information
Information is data that has meaning in some context for its receiver. When information is entered into and stored on a computer, it is generally referred to as data. After processing (such as formatting and printing), output data can again be perceived as information.

Information analysis
Information analysis provides a clear picture of how an organization handles information—how the information 'flows' through the organization.

Information management
Information management describes the means by which an organization efficiently plans, collects, organizes, uses, controls, disseminates and disposes of its information, and through which it ensures that the value of that information is identified and exploited to the fullest extent.

Information processing facilities
Any information processing system, service or infrastructure, or the physical locations housing them.

Information security
Information security is the protection of information from a wide range of threats in order to ensure business continuity, minimize business risk, and maximize return on investments and business opportunities.

Information security event

An information security event is an identified occurrence of a system, service or network state indicating a possible breach of information security policy or failure of safeguards, or a previously unknown situation that may be security-relevant.
[ISO/IEC TR 18044:2004]

Information security incident

An information security incident is indicated by a single or series of unwanted or unexpected information security events that have a significant probability of compromising business operations and threatening information security.
[ISO/IEC TR 18044:2004]

Information security management

Coordinated activities to direct and control an organization with regard to risk. Risk management typically includes risk assessment, risk treatment, risk acceptance and risk communication.
[ISO/IEC Guide 73:2002]

Information system

In a very broad sense, the term information system is frequently used to refer to the interaction between people, processes, data and technology. In this sense, the term is used to refer not only to the information and communication technology (ICT) an organization uses, but also to the way in which people interact with this technology in support of business processes.

Integrity

The concept of integrity ensures that unauthorized modification to software and hardware is prevented, unauthorized modification is not made to data by authorized and unauthorized personnel and/or processes and that data is internally and externally consistent.

Policy

The overall intention and direction as formally expressed by management.

Risk

A combination of the probability of an event and its consequence.

Risk analysis

The systematic use of information to identify sources and to estimate the risk.

Risk assessment

The overall process of risk analysis and risk evaluation.

Risk evaluation

The process of comparing the estimated risk against given risk criteria to determine the significance of the risk.

Risk treatment

The process of selection and implementation of measures to modify risk.

Third party

The person or body that is recognized as being independent of the parties involved, as far as the issue in question is concerned.
[ISO/IEC Guide 2:1996]

Threat

A potential cause of an unwanted incident, which may result in harm to a system or organization.
[ISO/IEC 13335-1:2004]

Vulnerability

A weakness of an asset or group of assets that can be exploited by one or more threats.

4. Information, security and architecture

Information security is achieved by implementing a suitable set of controls, including policies, processes, procedures, organizational structures and software and hardware functions. These controls need to be established, implemented, monitored, reviewed and improved, where necessary, to ensure that the specific security and business objectives of the organization are met. This should be done in conjunction with other business management processes.

'The process approach for **information security management** presented in the ISO 27002, Code of practice for information security encompasses the importance of:
a) understanding an organization's information security requirements and the need to establish policy and objectives for information security;
b) implementing and operating controls to manage an organization's information security risks in the context of the organization's overall business risks;
c) monitoring and reviewing the performance and effectiveness of the Information Security Management System ISMS; and
d) continual improvement based on objective measurement.'

Information and the supporting processes, systems, and networks are important business assets. Defining, achieving, maintaining, and improving information security may be essential to maintain competitive edge, cash flow, profitability, legal compliance, and commercial image.

Organizations and their information systems and networks are faced with security threats from a wide range of sources, including computer-assisted fraud, espionage, sabotage, vandalism, fire or flood. Causes of damage such as malicious code, computer hacking, and denial-of-service attacks have become more common, more ambitious, and increasingly sophisticated.

Information security is important to both public and private sector businesses, and to protect critical infrastructures. In both of these sectors information security will function as an enabler, e.g. to achieve e-government or e-business, and to avoid or reduce relevant risks.

The interconnection of public and private networks and the sharing of information resources increases the difficulty of achieving access control.

4.1 Fundamental principles of security

The definitions of confidentiality, integrity and availability have already been explained. Now we take a look more in depth.

A security program may have several large and small objectives, but the most important principles in all security programs are **confidentiality** (exclusivity), **integrity and availability**. These are referred to as the CIA triangle. The level of security required to accomplish these principles differs for each company, because each has its own unique combination of business and security goals and requirements. All security controls, mechanisms, and safeguards are implemented to provide one or more of these principles, and all risks, threats, and vulnerabilities are measured for their potential capability to compromise one or all of the CIA principles. Figure 4.1 illustrates the CIA triangle.

Confidentiality, integrity and availability are critical principles of security.

You should understand their meaning, how they are provided by different mechanisms, and how their absence can negatively affect an environment, all of which help you to best identify problems and provide proper solutions.

4.1.1 Confidentiality

Confidentiality, also called exclusivity, refers to the limits in terms of who can get what kind of information. For example, executives may be concerned with protecting their enterprise's strategic plans from competitors; individuals, on the other hand, are concerned about unauthorized access to their financial records.

Confidentiality ensures that the necessary level of secrecy is enforced at each element of data processing and prevents unauthorized disclosure. This level of confidentiality should prevail while data resides on systems and devices within the network, when it is transmitted, and once it reaches its destination.

Confidentiality can be provided by encrypting data as it is stored and transmitted, by using network traffic padding, strict access control, and data classification, and by training personnel on the proper procedures.

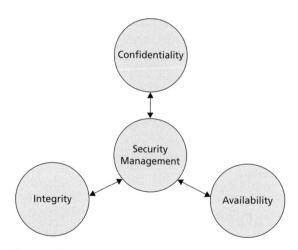

Figure 4.1 The CIA triangle

Examples of confidentiality measures are:
- Access to information is granted on a need to know basis. It is not necessary, for example, for a payroll employee to be able to see reports of discussions with the customer;
- Employees take measures to ensure that information does not find its way to those people who

do not need it. They ensure, for example, that no confidential documents are lying on their desk while they are away (clear desk policy);

- Logical access management ensures that unauthorized persons or processes do not have access to automated systems, databases and programs. A user, for example, does not have the right to change the settings of the PC;
- A separation of duties is created between the system development organization, the processing organization and the user organization. A system developer cannot, for example, make any changes to salaries;
- Strict separations are created between the development environment, the test and acceptance environment, and the production environment;
- In the processing and use of data, measures are taken to ensure the privacy of personnel and third parties. The Human Resources department (HR) may have, for example, its own network drive that is not accessible to other departments.

The use of computers by end users is surrounded with measures so that the confidentiality of the information is guaranteed.

An example is authentication of authorized users by means of a combination of userID, password and, sometimes, a 'challenge response token' that creates a one-time-password for every login session, which gives access to the computer and the network.
Network layers are encrypted, reducing the opportunity for traffic analysis. It is still possible in those circumstances for an attacker to assess the amount of traffic on a network and to observe the amount of traffic entering and leaving each end system. A countermeasure to this type of attack is traffic padding.

Traffic padding produces cipher text output continuously, even in the absence of plain text. A continuous random data stream is generated. When plain text is available, it is encrypted and transmitted. When input plaintext is not present, random data is encrypted and transmitted. This makes it impossible for an attacker to distinguish between true data flow and padding, and therefore impossible to deduce the amount of traffic.

Traffic padding is essentially a link encryption function. If only end-to-end encryption is employed, then the measures available to the defender are more limited. If encryption is implemented at the application layer, then an opponent can determine transport layer, network-layer addresses and traffic patterns which all remain accessible.

4.1.2 Integrity
Integrity refers to being correct or consistent with the intended state of information. Any unauthorized modification of data, whether deliberate or accidental, is a breach of data integrity. For example, data stored on disk is expected to be stable – it is are not supposed to be changed at random by problems with the disk controllers. Similarly, application programs are supposed to record information correctly and not introduce deviations from the intended values.

Donn Parker explains this as follows: *"My definition of information integrity comes from the dictionaries. Integrity means that the information is whole, sound, and unimpaired (not necessarily correct). It means nothing is missing from the information, it is complete and in intended good order.*" The author's statement comes close in saying that the information is in a correct...state. Information may be incorrect or not authentic but have integrity or correct and authentic but lacking in integrity.

Environments that enforce and provide this attribute of security ensure that attackers, or mistakes by users, do not compromise the integrity of systems or data. When an attacker inserts a virus, logic bomb[3], or backdoor[4] into a system, the system's integrity is compromised. This can, in turn, negatively affect the integrity of information held on the system by corruption, malicious modification, or replacement of data with incorrect data. Strict access controls, intrusion detection[5], and hashing[6] can combat these threats.

Users usually affect a system or its data's integrity by mistake (although internal users may also commit malicious deeds). For example, a user with a full hard drive may unwittingly delete configuration files under the mistaken assumption that deleting a boot.ini file[7] must be okay because they don't remember ever using it. Or, for example, a user may insert incorrect values into a data processing application that ends up charging a customer $3,000,000 instead of $300. Incorrectly modifying data kept in databases is another common way that users accidentally corrupt data, a mistake that can have lasting effects.

Integrity measures are:
• Changes in systems and data are authorized. For example, one member of staff enters in a new price for an article on the website, and another verifies the correctness of that price before it is published;
• Where possible, mechanisms are built in that force people to use the correct term. For example, a customer is always called a 'customer', the term 'client' cannot be entered into the database;
• Users' actions are recorded (logged) so that it can be determined who made a change in the information;
• Vital system actions, for example installing new software, cannot be carried out by just one person. By segregating duties, positions and authorities, at least two people will be necessary to carry out a change that has major consequences.

The integrity of data can be ensured to a large degree through encryption techniques, which protects the information from unauthorized access or change. The policy and management principles for encryption can be defined in a separate policy document.

---

3   A logic bomb is a piece of code intentionally inserted into a software system that will set off a malicious function when specified conditions are met. For example, a programmer may hide a piece of code that starts deleting files (such as a salary database trigger), should they ever be terminated from the company.

4   A backdoor in a computer system (or cryptosystem or algorithm) is a method of bypassing normal authentication, securing remote access to a computer, obtaining access to plaintext, and so on, while attempting to remain undetected. The backdoor may take the form of an installed program (e.g., Back Orifice), or could be a modification to an existing program or hardware device.

5   Intrusion detection (ID) is a type of security management system for computers and networks. An ID system gathers and analyzes information from various areas within a computer or a network to identify possible security breaches, which include both intrusions (attacks from outside the organization) and misuse (attacks from within the organization). ID uses *vulnerability assessment* (sometimes referred to as *scanning*), which is a technology developed to assess the security of a computer system or network.

6   Hashing is the transformation of a string of characters into a usually shorter fixed-length value or key that represents the original string. Hashing is used to index and retrieve items in a database because it is faster to find the item using the shorter hashed key than to find it using the original value. It is also used in many encryption algorithms.

7   boot.ini is a file on a computer which contains configuration options for a boot menu. Without this file, or a corrupted file, the computer will not start again.

4.1.3 Availability

The characteristics of availability are:
- Timeliness - the information is available when needed;
- Continuity - the staff can carry on working in the event of a failure;
- Robustness - there is sufficient capacity to allow all staff on the system to work.

For example, a disk crash or denial-of-service attack both cause a breach of availability. Any delay that exceeds the expected service levels for a system can be described as a breach of availability. System availability can be affected by device or software failure. Back-up devices[8] should be used and available to quickly replace critical systems, and employees should be skilled and available to make the necessary adjustments to bring the system back online. Environmental issues like heat, cold, humidity, static electricity, and contaminants can also affect system availability. Systems should be protected from these elements, properly grounded electrically, and closely monitored. Denial-of-service (DoS) attacks are popular methods for hackers to disrupt a company's system availability and productivity. These attacks are mounted to reduce the ability of users to access system resources and information. To protect against these attacks, only the necessary services and ports should be available on systems, and intrusion detection systems (IDS) should monitor the network traffic and host activities.

Certain firewall and router configurations can also reduce the threat of DoS attacks and possibly stop them from occurring.

Examples of availability measures include:
- The management and storage of data is such that the risk of losing information is minimal. Data is, for example, stored on a network disk, not on the hard disk of the PC;
- Back-up procedures are set up. The statutory requirements for how long data must be stored are taken into account. The location of the back-up is separated physically from the business in order to ensure the availability in cases of emergency;
- Statutory requirements for how long data must be stored will vary from country to country in EU, the USA, and elsewhere. It is important to check the individual government regulatory agencies for specific requirements.

Emergency procedures are set up to ensure that the activities can recommence as soon as possible after a large-scale disruption.

4.2 Parkerian hexad [9]

The Parkerian hexad is a set of six elements of information security proposed by Donn B. Parker. The term was coined by M. E. Kabay. The Parkerian hexad adds three additional attributes to the three classic security attributes of the CIA triangle (confidentiality, integrity, availability).

---

8   In information technology, a back-up or the process of backing-up refers to making copies of data so that these additional copies may be used to restore the original after a data loss event. These additional copies are typically called "back-ups." The verb is back up in two words, whereas the noun is back-up (often used like an adjective in compound nouns.

9   http://en.wikipedia.org/wiki/Parkerian_Hexad

The attributes of the Parkerian hexad are as follows:
1. Confidentiality;
2. Possession or control;
3. Integrity;
4. Authenticity;
5. Availability;
6. Utility.

These attributes of information are atomic in that they are not broken down into further constituents; they are non-overlapping in that they refer to unique aspects of information. Any information security breach can be described as affecting one or more of these fundamental attributes of information. Confidentiality, integrity and availability have all been mentioned before.

4.2.1 Possession or control

Suppose a thief were to steal a sealed envelope containing a bank debit card and (foolishly) its personal identification number. Even if the thief did not open that envelope, the victim of the theft would be legitimately concerned that the thief could use the card fraudulently at any time without the control of the owner. That situation illustrates a loss of control or possession of information but does not involve the breach of confidentiality.

4.2.2 Authenticity

Authenticity refers to the veracity of the claim of origin or authorship of the information. For example, one method of verifying the authorship of a hand written document is to compare the handwriting characteristics of the document to a sample of others which have already been verified. For electronic information, a digital signature could be used to verify the authorship of a digital document using public-key cryptography (this could also be used to verify the integrity of the document).

4.2.3 Utility

Utility means usefulness. For example, suppose someone encrypted data on a disk to prevent unauthorized access or undetected modifications – and then lost the decryption key: that would be a breach of utility. The data would be confidential, controlled, integral, authentic, and available – it just wouldn't be useful in that form. Similarly, conversion of salary data from one currency into an inappropriate currency would be a breach of utility, as would the storage of data in a format inappropriate for a specific computer architecture; e.g., EBCDIC instead of ASCII or 9-track magnetic tape instead of DVD-ROM. A tabular representation of data substituted for a graph could be described as a breach of utility if the substitution made it more difficult to interpret the data. Utility is often confused with availability because breaches such as those described in these examples may also require time to work around the change in data format or presentation. However, the concept of usefulness is distinct from that of availability.

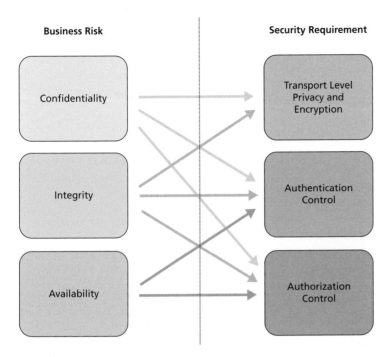

Figure 4.2 Mapping business risk – security requirements

4.3 Due care and due diligence

Due diligence and due care are becoming serious issues in computer operations today. In fact the legal system has begun to hold major partners liable for the lack of due care in the event of a major security breach. Violations of security and privacy are hot issues that are confronting the Internet community, and standards covering the best practices of due care are necessary for an organization's protection.

What does due diligence and due care mean?

'Due diligence is the act of investigating and understanding the risks the company (or governmental organization) faces. A company practices due care by developing and implementing security policies, procedures, and standards.'

'Due care shows that a company has taken responsibility for the activities that take place within the corporation and has taken the necessary steps to help protect the company, its resources, and employees from possible threats.'

So, due diligence is about understanding the current threats and risks, and due care is implementing countermeasures to provide protection from those threats. If a company does not practice due care and due diligence pertaining to the security of its assets, it can be legally charged with negligence and held accountable for any ramifications of that negligence according to the laws of every country in which it operates, if it is a business.

4.4   Information

4.4.1   Difference between data and information

It is essential to understand the difference between data and information. Data can be processed by information technology, but it becomes information once it has acquired a certain meaning. In our daily life we come across information in countless various forms. Information can take the form of text, but also of the spoken word and video images. When it comes to information security you must take into account the diverse forms in which information can primarily focus on. It involves, after all, the security of the information itself and is independent of the way it is presented. The way information is presented, however, imposes some restrictions on the measures that are necessary to protect that information.

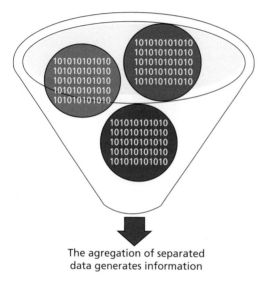

The agregation of separated
data generates information

Figure 4.3 Aggregation of data generates information

4.4.2   Information analysis

Information analysis provides a clear picture of how an organization handles information—how the information 'flows' through the organization. For example, a guest registers with a hotel through the website. This information is passed on to the online booking system, which then allocates a room. The reception knows that the guest will arrive today. The domestic services department knows that the room must be clean for the guest's arrival. In all these steps, it is important that the information is reliable.

4.4.3   Informatics

'Informatics is converting data into information. Humming a tune and your search engine correcting the pitch, predicting the spread of the next flu epidemic, combating a malicious hacker, understanding the human genome and exploring virtual reality. Supporting cutting edge research, developing business solutions and more…'

Informatics develops new uses for information technology, is interested in how people transform technology, and how technology transforms us.

4.4.4 Value of data

Data can have great significance – depending on how it is used – even if it isn't in the format of 'information' as defined earlier. There would be no need for 'data protection' and hence 'computer security' if data by definition had no significance. The value of data is determined primarily by the user.

4.4.5 Value of information

As mentioned earlier, information is knowledge that someone has acquired. While some people may consider a particular set of data uninteresting, others may be able to extract valuable information from it. The value of information is, therefore, determined by the value that the recipient attaches to it.

4.4.6 Information as a production factor

The standard production factors of a company or organization are capital, (manual) labor and raw materials. In information technology, it is common to also regard information as a production factor. Businesses cannot exist without information. A warehouse that loses its customer and stock information would usually not be able to operate without it. For some businesses, such as an accountant's office, information is actually their only product.

4.4.7 Information systems

The transfer and processing of information takes place via an information system infrastructure. It should be pointed out that an information system is not necessarily the same as an IT system (information technology system).

In a very broad sense, the term information system is frequently used to refer to the interaction between people, processes, data and technology. In this sense, the term is used to refer not only to the information and communication technology (ICT) an organization uses, but also to the way in which people interact with this technology in support of business processes[10].

Examples of information systems are files in file cabinets[11], computer files and databases, mobile telephones and printers. In the context of information security, an information system is the entire combination of means, procedures, rules and people that ensure the information supply for an operational process.

ICT components include:
- Workstations, which consists of the PC with the operating system software and other software;
- Data transport via a network, cabled or wireless;
- Servers, consisting of the server with an operating system and software;
- Data storage, for example disk space, email and databases;
- Mobile phones evolve more and more to small computer devices with large removable storage capacity and the possibility to exchange information by mobile network and/or Bluetooth connections.

---

10   Kroenke, D M. (2008). Experiencing MIS. Prentice-Hall, Upper Saddle River, NJ
11   A file cabinet is a piece of office furniture usually used to store paper documents in file folders.

4.5   Information management

'Information management describes the means by which an organization efficiently plans, collects, organizes, uses, controls, disseminates and disposes of its information, and through which it ensures that the value of that information is identified and exploited to the fullest extent.'

When you translate this definition into usable English you could say that this interdisciplinary field draws on and combines skills and resources from:
* librarianship and information science;
* information technology;
* records management;
* archives and general management.

Its focus is information as a resource, independently of the physical form in which it occurs. Books and periodicals, data stored on local or remote computers, microforms, audio-visual media and the information in people's heads are all within its scope. Some of the main topics practitioners are concerned with are:
* classification and coding;
* subject indexing;
* construction and use of thesauri and controlled vocabularies;
* cataloguing and indexing by names, places, and events;
* database design and data structures;
* physical storage of books and records, in paper and electronic form;
* storage of photographic and digitized images;
* information audits: reviews of an organization's information resources;
* documentation of museum objects, both for management purposes and as a resource for scholarship.

4.6   Secure information systems design

Many information systems have not been designed to be secure. The security that can be achieved through technical means is limited, and should be supported by appropriate management and procedures. Identifying which controls should be in place requires careful planning and attention to detail. Information security management requires, as a minimum, participation by all employees in the organization. It may also require participation from shareholders, suppliers, third parties, customers or other external parties. Specialist advice from outside organizations may also be needed.

Information security management establishes the foundation for a comprehensive security program to ensure the protection of the organization's information assets. Today organizations are highly interconnected via the Internet. Virtually no organization can claim to have so called 'stand-alone' computer systems. Sometimes an organization has a strict separation between the Internet and the corporate network. Even then, often one or more Internet connections are established.

This makes it necessary to understand the risks for the business and how to deal with these. The risk manager has to understand the business objectives and must know how to mitigate the risks for the business in such a way that the business can implement security countermeasures without these being a burden to the business.

Information security encompasses the administrative, technical and physical controls necessary to protect the confidentiality, integrity and availability of information assets. The controls are manifested through the implementation of policies, procedures, standards and guidelines.

4.6.1 Distributed computing

The trend to *distributed computing* has also weakened the effectiveness of central, specialist control. In general, distributed computing is any computing that involves multiple computers remote from each other, where each has a role in a computation problem or information processing.

In business enterprises, distributed computing generally has meant putting various steps in business processes at the most efficient places in a network of computers. In the typical transaction the user interface processing is done in the PC at the user's location, business processing is done in a remote computer, and database access and processing is done in another computer that provides centralized access for many business processes. Typically, this kind of distributed computing uses the client/server communications model.

The Distributed Computing Environment (DCE) is a widely-used industry standard that supports this kind of distributed computing. On the Internet, third-party service providers now offer some generalized services that fit into this model.

A directory service has a hierarchical database of users, computers, printers, resources, and attributes of each. The directory is mainly used for look-up operations, which enable users to track down resources and other users. The administrator can then develop access control, security, and auditing policies that dictate who can access these objects, how the objects can be accessed, and audit each of these actions

More recently, distributed computing is used to refer to any large collaboration in which many individual personal computer owners allow some of their computer's processing time to be put at the service of a large problem. The best-known example is the SETI@home project in which individual computer owners can volunteer some of their multitasking processing cycles (while concurrently still using their computer) to the Search for Extraterrestrial Intelligence (SETI) project. This computing-intensive problem uses your computer (and thousands of others) to download and search radio telescope data.

4.7 Operational processes and information

Management covers a very wide range of activities designed to improve the effectiveness and efficiency of an organization. To understand the full rage of management actions, and to develop the knowledge and skill to perform these management activities well, we can classify the complete range of management activities in different ways. One such way of classifying management activities is based on the dimensions of totality of the organizational performance that is being focused on. To manage an organization effectively, managers need to focus on the whole organization as a single unit. At the same time they also need to pay individual attention to each small activity performed by many smaller units within the organization.

By classifying management in terms of the totality of the organizational performance, we can define a continuum of management levels ranging from strategic management on one end, to operational management at the other. Strategic management concentrates on the performance of the complete organization. The focus here is to determine the most appropriate objectives that the organization should pursue given its internal strengths and weaknesses as well as the external opportunities and threats faced by it.

Strategic management involves achieving a balance between the requirements of the different functions and units of the organization. It also involves balancing risks in both the short and long term. Based on these considerations, strategic management determines the long term objectives to be pursued by the organization and identifies the ways and means of achieving these objectives. One unique characteristic of strategic management is the absence of any higher level plans or objectives to guide strategic management action.

Operational management lies at the other end of the continuum of management levels. It is concerned with ensuring that the day-to-day operations of the organization are carried out effectively and efficiently. For example, operational management will concentrate on ensuring that workmen on the shop floor are instructed correctly on the jobs to be performed by them at any particular time and that they are provided with the required material, tools and other facilities to get on with the work.

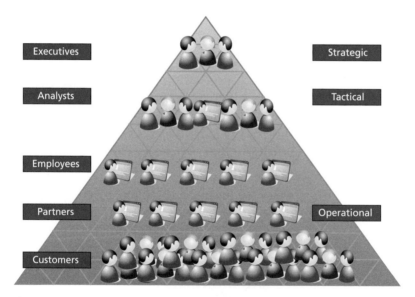

Figure 4.4 Classifying management in terms of organizational performance

The level between the strategic and operational management is the tactical management level. This level of management is concerned with planning and control for individual organizational functions such as marketing, production, and HRD, or sub-functions within them, aimed at improving performance in the short to medium term.[12]

At the business process level things happen in much the same way as previously described. Each business method is a collection of related, structured activities or tasks that produce a specific service or product (serve a particular goal) for a particular customer or customers. It often can be shown by means of a flowchart as a sequence of activities.

---

12   http://www.enotes.com/business/q-and-a/discuss-difference-between-strategic-tactical-97313

A business process begins with a customer's need and ends with the fulfillment of these needs. Process-oriented organizations break down the barriers of structural departments and try to avoid functional silos.

A business process can be decomposed into several sub-processes, which have their own attributes, but also contribute to achieving the goal of the super-process. The analysis of business processes typically includes the mapping of processes and sub-processes down to the activity level.
Business processes are designed to add value for the customer and should not include unnecessary activities. The outcome of a well designed business process is increased effectiveness (value for the customer) and increased efficiency (less costs for the company).

Business processes can be modeled through a large number of methods and techniques. For instance, the Business Process Modeling Notation is a business process modeling technique that can be used, for example, to draw a book selling business process in terms of a simple workflow.

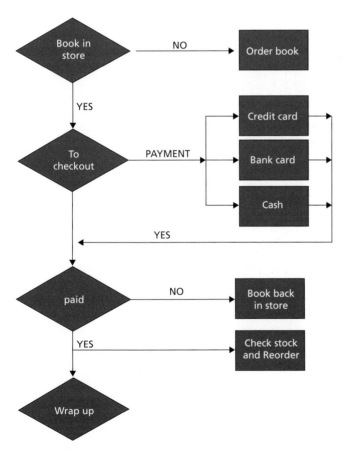

Figure 4.5 Example of a simple flowchart

4.8 Information architecture

Information security is closely related to information architecture. When designing information systems it is necessary to think about information security from the very beginning. This section gives a brief description about information architecture.

The definition of an architecture used in ANSI/IEEE Standard 1471-2000 is:

'The fundamental organization of a system, embodied in its components, their relationships to each other and the environment, and the principles governing its design and evolution.'"

TOGAF is an architecture framework - The Open Group Architecture Framework. It enables you to design, evaluate, and build the right architecture for your organization.

The key to TOGAF is the Architecture Development Method (ADM) - a reliable, proven method for developing an IT enterprise architecture that meets the needs of your business.

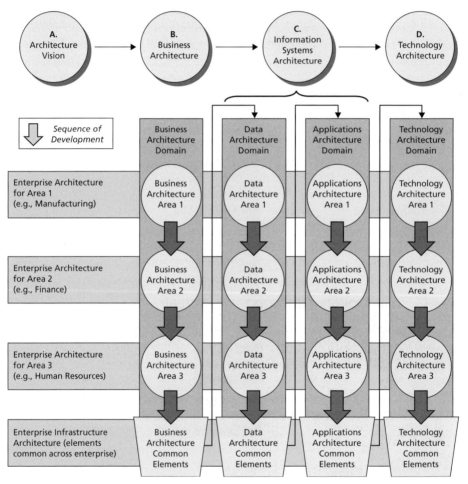

Figure 4.6 Different TOGAF architecture areas

Information architecture (IA)[13] is the art of expressing a model or concept of information used in activities that require explicit details of complex systems. Among these activities are

---

library systems, content management systems, web development, user interactions, database development, programming, technical writing and critical system software design. Information architecture has somewhat different meanings in these different branches of IS or IT architecture. Most definitions have common qualities: a structural design of shared environments, methods of organizing and labeling websites, intranets, and online communities, and ways of bringing the principles of design and architecture to the digital landscape.

Historically the term 'information architect' is attributed to Richard Saul Wurman. Wurman sees architecture as "used in the words architect of foreign policy. I mean architect as in the creating of systemic, structural, and orderly principles to make something work - the thoughtful making of either artifact, or idea, or policy that informs because it is clear."

Organizing functionality and content into a structure that people are able to navigate intuitively doesn't happen by chance. Organizations must recognize the importance of information architecture or else they run the risk of creating great content and functionality that no one can ever find. It also discusses the relationship between information architecture and usability, in the context of real-world projects.

Computer systems can be frustrating because they do not always perform as the user wants. People using systems become frustrated because they simply are not capable of doing what they want to do. But technology has progressed and now technology can do practically whatever people want. So why doesn't everyone using a computer have a large smile on their face?

The shear wealth of functionality and information has become the new problem. The challenge facing organizations is how to guide people through the vast amount of information on offer, so they can successfully find the information they want and thus find value in the system?

An effective information architecture enables people to step logically through a system confident they are getting closer to the information they require. Most people only notice information architecture when it is poor and stops them from finding the information they require.

Information architecture is most commonly associated with websites and intranets, but it can be used in the context of any information structures or computer systems.

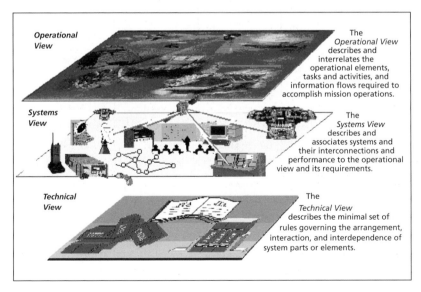

Operational View

The *Operational View* describes and interrelates the operational elements, tasks and activities, and information flows required to accomplish mission operations.

Systems View

The *Systems View* describes and associates systems and their interconnections and performance to the operational view and its requirements.

Technical View

The *Technical View* describes the minimal set of rules governing the arrangement, interaction, and interdependence of system parts or elements.

Figure 4.7 TOGAF views

4.8.1 The evolution of information architecture

Richard Saul Wurman, who coined the term 'information architecture' trained as an architect, but became interested in the way information is gathered, organized and presented to convey meaning. Wurman's initial definition of information architecture was "organizing the patterns in data, making the complex clear".

The term was largely dormant until in 1996 it was seized upon by a couple of library scientists, Lou Rosenfeld and Peter Morville. They used the term to define the work they were doing in structuring large-scale websites and intranets.

In '*Information Architecture for the World Wide Web: Designing Large-Scale Web Sites*' they define information architecture as:

- The combination of organization, labeling, and navigation schemes within an information system;
- The structural design of an information space to facilitate task completion and intuitive access to content;
- The art and science of structuring and classifying web sites and intranets to help people find and manage information;
- An emerging discipline and community of practice focused on bringing principles of design and architecture to the digital landscape.

Today Wurman's influence on information architecture is fairly minimal, but many of the metaphors used to describe the discipline echo the work done by architects. For example, information architecture is described as the blueprint that developers and designers use to build the system.

4.9 Summary

In this chapter you have learned about the various forms of information and information systems. You have also been introduced to the important trio: availability, confidentiality and integrity. Finally, you have seen how information security is important for the operational processes, the information architecture and information management.

4.10 Springbooks

As was mentioned in chapter 2, Springbooks started as a small bookstore, but over time evolved into a large company with a lot of bookstores. As a consequence, the total volume of books and their associated stock requirements increased accordingly.

Springbooks international has a lot of information to deal with. Some books are popular in all countries and others just in a specific country.

Popular books shall be in stock all the time. Popular books are delivered in a short time. Unsold magazines must be sent back to the publisher. Customer information is shared with other Springbooks stores but not shared with partners of Springbooks. All these streams of information must be in compliance with local and international (privacy) laws and are crucial for the least expensive cost to the organization.

Your job is to recognize the most important security issues, dealing with information management. Make an information architecture 'picture' (written and/or drawn) to show the flow of information between the local and international bookstores. Separate national and international shared information, and show and explain why some information cannot be shared with other countries e.q. headquarters.

Based on Springbooks, give a short description of the most important stream of information sources to recognize in a (international) bookstore and the security issues that are most important for an international bookstore. Remember the chapter about the organization of Springbooks and think in terms of the three main pillars of information security:
* confidentiality;
* integrity;
* availability.

5. Security management

5.1 Security definitions

To understand how security can be managed, a number of important concepts must first be explained. 'Vulnerability','threat', 'risk' and 'exposure' are often used to represent the same thing even though they have different meanings and relationships to each other. It is important to understand each word's definition, but more importantly to understand its relationship to the other concepts.

Before we start defining a security strategy, we need to know what we are protecting and what we are proctecting it from. The methodology we employ to help us acquire some insight into this is called *risk analysis*. There are various ways of performing a risk analysis. We will discuss a number in this chapter.

Security requirements are identified by a methodical assessment of security risks. Expenditure on controls needs to be balanced against the business harm likely to result from security failures.

The results of the risk assessment will help to guide and determine the appropriate management action and priorities for managing information security risks, and for implementing controls selected to protect against risks and threats.

Risk assessment (risk analysis) should be repeated periodically to address any changes that might influence the risk assessment results.

5.1.1 Vulnerability

A vulnerability is a weakness of an asset or group of assets that can be exploited by one or more threats. A vulnerability characterizes the absence or weakness of a safeguard that could be exploited. This vulnerability may be a service running on a server, unpatched applications or operating system software, unrestricted modem dial-in access, an open port on a firewall, lax physical security that allows anyone to enter a server room, or non-enforced password management on servers and workstations.

5.1.2 Threat

A threat is a potential cause of an unwanted incident, which may result in harm to a system or organization. The entity that takes advantage of a vulnerability is referred to as a threat agent. A threat agent could be an intruder accessing the network through a port on the firewall, a process accessing data in a way that violates the security policy, a tornado wiping out a facility, or an employee making an unintentional mistake that could expose confidential information or destroy a file's integrity. Threats differ in each country depending on the level of development and Internet use. Information security is important to governments, academia, military, healthcare, etc. Terrorism and war are security threats too.

5.1.3 Risk

A risk is the likelihood of a threat agent taking advantage of a vulnerability and the corresponding business impact. If a firewall has several ports open, there is a higher likelihood that an intruder will use one to access the network in an unauthorized way. If users are not educated on processes and procedures, there is a higher likelihood that an employee will make an intentional or unintentional mistake that may destroy data. If an Intrusion Detection System[14] is not implemented on a network, there is a higher likelihood that an attack will go unnoticed until it is too late. Risk ties the vulnerability, threat, and likelihood of exploitation to the resulting business impact.

In practice
- A fire can break out at your company;
- An employee who does not work at the HR department gains access to private or sensitive information;
- Someone appears as an employee and tries to gain information;
- Your company is hit by a power failure;
- A hacker manages to gain access to the company's IT network.

5.1.4 Exposure
An exposure is an instance of being exposed to losses from a threat agent. A vulnerability exposes an organization to possible damages. If password management is lax and password rules are not enforced, the company is exposed to the possibility of having users' passwords captured and used in an unauthorized manner. If a company does not have its wiring inspected and does not put proactive fire prevention steps into place, it exposes itself to potentially devastating fires.

5.1.5 A countermeasure, or safeguard
A countermeasure is put into place to mitigate against the potential risk. It may be a software configuration, a hardware device, or procedure that eliminates a vulnerability or reduces the likelihood that a threat agent will be able to exploit a vulnerability. Examples of countermeasures include strong password management, a security guard, access control mechanisms within an operating system, the implementation of basic input/output system (BIOS) passwords, and security-awareness training.

If a company has anti-virus software but does not keep the virus signatures up-to-date, this is a vulnerability. The company is vulnerable to virus attacks. The threat is that a virus will show up in the environment and disrupt productivity. The likelihood of a virus showing up in the environment and causing damage is the risk. If a virus infiltrates the company's environment, then a vulnerability has been exploited and the company is exposed to loss. The countermeasure in this situation is to prevent against a virus attack by installing anti-virus software on all computers and, of course, keeping the anti-virus signatures up to date.

5.2   Assessing security risks
Risk assessments should identify, quantify, and prioritize risks against criteria for risk acceptance and objectives that are relevant to the organization. The results should guide and determine the appropriate management action and priorities for managing information security risks and for implementing controls selected to protect against these risks. The process of assessing risks and

---

14   An intrusion detection system (IDS) inspects all inbound and outbound network activity and identifies suspicious patterns that may indicate a network or system attack from someone attempting to break into or compromise a system.

selecting controls may need to be performed a number of times to cover different parts of the organization or individual information systems.

Risk assessment should include the systematic approach of estimating the magnitude of risks (risk analysis) and the process of comparing the estimated risks against risk criteria to determine the significance of the risks (risk evaluation).

Risk assessments should also be performed periodically to address changes in the security requirements and in the risk situation, e.g. in the assets, threats, vulnerabilities, impacts, the risk evaluation, and when significant changes occur. These risk assessments should be undertaken in a methodical manner capable of producing comparable and reproducible results.

The information security risk assessment should have a clearly defined scope in order to be effective and should include relationships with risk assessments in other areas, if appropriate. The scope of a risk assessment can be either the whole organization, parts of the organization, an individual information system, specific system components, or services where this is practicable, realistic, and helpful.

5.3 Mitigating security risks

In this section we consider why controls are important countermeasures in safeguarding information.

5.3.1 Controls

"Security controls are measures taken to safeguard an information system from attacks against the confidentiality, integrity, and availability (CIA) of the information system. Note that the terms safeguard and countermeasure are sometimes used as synonyms for security control."
(Tijdelijkebronaanduiding3) http://www.giac.org/resources/whitepaper/operations/205.php

5.3.2 Considering the treatment of a risk

Before considering the treatment of a risk, the organization should decide upon the criteria for determining whether or not risks can be accepted. A risk may be accepted if, for example, it is assessed that the risk is low or that the cost of treatment is not cost-effective for the organization. Such decisions should be recorded.

A risk handling decision needs to be made for each of the risks identified following the risk assessment. Possible controls for risk treatment include:
- Applying appropriate controls to reduce the risks;
- Knowingly and objectively accepting risks, providing they clearly satisfy the organization's policy and criteria for risk acceptance;
- Avoiding risks by not allowing actions that would cause the risks to occur;
- Transferring the associated risks to other parties, e.g. insurers or suppliers.

For those risks where the risk treatment decision has been to apply appropriate controls, then these controls:
- Should be selected and implemented to meet the requirements identified by a risk assessment.

Controls should ensure that risks are reduced to an acceptable level taking into account:
- Requirements and constraints of national and international legislation and regulations;
- Organizational objectives;
- Operational requirements and constraints;
- The cost of implementation and operation in relation to the risks being reduced, and remaining proportional to the organization's requirements and constraints;
- The need to balance the investment in implementation and operation of controls against the harm likely to result from security failures.

Controls can be selected from the ISO 27002 standard or from other control sets, your company use, or new controls can be designed to meet the specific needs of the organization. It is necessary to recognize that some controls may not be applicable to every information system or environment, and might not be practicable for all organizations.

It may not be possible for smaller organizations to segregate all duties, and other ways of achieving the same control objective may be necessary.

It should be kept in mind that no set of controls can achieve complete security, and that additional management action should be implemented to monitor, evaluate, and improve the efficiency and effectiveness of security controls to support the organization's aims.

When a threat manifests itself, such as when a hacker manages to get access to the company network, we call that an *incident*. A power failure, like the power-losses in Brazil in 2008 and 2009 are large incidents which can threaten the survival of the responsible electricity company. We refer to this as a *disaster*.

When a threat materializes, a risk for the organization arises. Both the extent of the risk and management's assessment determine whether measures have to be taken in order to minimize the risk and what they may be.

The path from threats to risks and then to security measures is called risk management.

5.4   Risk management

'Risk management is the process of planning, organizing, leading, and controlling the activities of an organization in order to minimize the effects of risk on an organization's capital and earnings.'[15]

5.4.1   Security organization

Risks can come from uncertainty in financial markets, project failures, legal liabilities, credit risk, accidents, natural causes and disasters as well as deliberate attacks from an adversary. Several risk management standards have been developed, including those from the Project Management Institute, the National Institute of Science and Technology (NIST), actuarial societies, and ISO standards. Methods, definitions and goals vary widely according to whether the risk management method is in the context of project management, security, engineering, industrial processes, financial portfolios, actuarial assessments, or public health and safety.

---

15   http://searchcio.techtarget.com/sDefinition/0,,sid182_gci508983,00.htm

The risk strategy may include transferring the risk to another party, avoiding the risk, reducing the negative effect of the risk, and accepting some or all of the consequences of a particular risk. Risk management is an ongoing process that applies to all aspects of the operational processes. In large organizations, the task of monitoring this process is carried out by an information security specialist, such as an Information Security Officer (ISO) or Chief Information Security Officer (CISO), who is appointed especially for this role and who is responsible to the highest level of management).

This chapter will explain how a risk analysis works in practice.

5.5   Risk analysis

'Risk analysis is the process of defining and analyzing the dangers to individuals, businesses and government agencies posed by potential natural and human-caused adverse events'.'

In IT, a risk analysis report can be used to align technology-related objectives with a company's business objectives. A risk analysis report can be either **quantitative** or **qualitative**.

In quantitative risk analysis, an attempt is made to numerically determine the probabilities of various adverse events and the likely extent of the losses if a particular event takes place.

Qualitative risk analysis, which is used more often, does not involve numerical probabilities or predictions of loss. Instead, the qualitative method involves defining the various threats, determining the extent of the vulnerabilities, and devising countermeasures should an attack occur.

The purpose of carrying out a risk analysis is to clarify which threats are relevant to the operational processes and to identify the associated risks. The appropriate security level, along with the associated security measures, can then be determined.

A risk analysis is used to ensure that the security measures are deployed in a cost-effective and timely manner, and consequently provide an effective answer to the threats.

Security as a state or condition is *resistance to harm.* From an objective perspective, it is a structure's actual (conceptual and never fully established) degree of resistance to harm. This means that the degree of resistance to harm can change day by day. That condition derives from the structure's relationship (vulnerability, distance, insulation, protection) to threats in its environment. From a subjective perspective, security is the perception or belief that a valued structure has sufficient objective security. The subjective meaning of security as 'freedom from anxiety or fear' resonates in the origins of the word. The Latin term 'Se-Cura' means literally 'without care' as in 'carefree'. Security as a form of protection is made up of *structures and processes that provide or improve security as a condition.* The Institute for Security and Open Methodologies (ISECOM) defines security as "a form of protection where a separation is created between the assets and the threat". This includes but is not limited to the elimination of either the asset or the threat. In order to be secure, either the asset is physically removed from the threat or the threat is physically removed from the asset.

Even for experienced security specialists it is not easy to find the right balance between security measures that are too stringent and those that are ineffective or inappropriate. A great deal of money is spent on unnecessary security measures because there is not a well thought-out security concept as a foundation. A risk analysis can prove a valuable aid in arriving at such a concept.

A risk analysis helps the business to correctly assess the risks and determine the correct and balanced security measures. Management can also identify the costs that are involved in taking the appropriate measures.
A risk analysis has four main objectives:
1. To identify assets and their value;
2. To determine vulnerabilities and threats;
3. To determine the risk that threats will become a reality and disrupt the operational process;
4. To determine a balance between the costs of an incident and the costs of a security measure.

Part of the risk analysis is a cost/benefit assessment. The annual costs associated with the security measures are compared with the potential losses that would occur if the threats were to become reality.
The organization must take care to avoid a situation where a server, including the data, is worth €100,000 and the security measures taken cost €150,000. That said, such situations do actually sometimes happen. Statutory requirements for protecting data can sometimes force companies to take measures that actually cost more than the value of the assets being protected.

In addition, it can be difficult to determine the value of data. Consider, for example, if Springbooks' customer database containing thousands of names, addresses and credit card information were to be disclosed in some unauthorized way; the damage to Springbooks' reputation would be huge. It is difficult to calculate the damage caused, but the trust of the customer in Springbooks would decrease immediately.
There are two main groups of risk analyses:
• quantitative risk analysis;
• qualitative risk analysis.

5.5.1 Quantitative risk analysis
A quantitative risk analysis aims to calculate, based on the risk impact, the level of the financial loss and the probability that a threat may become an incident. The value of each element in all operational processes is determined. These values can be made up of the costs of the security measures, as well as the value of property itself, including such items as buildings, hardware, software, information and business impact. The time spans before a threat appears, the effectiveness of security measures and the risk that a vulnerability will be exploited are also elements to be considered.
In this way, a clear picture is provided of the total financial risk and appropriate measures may be determined. An important part of this is determining which residual risks are acceptable to the managers responsible. The costs of the measures must not exceed the value of the protected object and the risk.
A purely quantitative risk analysis is practically impossible. A quantitative risk analysis tries to assign values to all aspects, but that is not always possible. A defective server can be assigned a value: for instance the purchase value and the depreciation of the server, the value of the software that has to be installed, and the cost of wages associated with any repairs can all be determined. But just try giving a value to the damage caused to a company. How much value loss does a

company suffer when certain data is lost? It may be possible to determine this on occasions, but certainly not always.

This can make it difficult to determine the correct measures for preventing damage.

In practice
- In an insurance office the details of policy holders become public through a fault of an employee. How many clients will be lost as a result?
- In a Law Court the personal details of witnesses are highly confidential to protect the witnesses against possible repercussions from criminals who due to give testimony against. If these personal details are leaked, how many people would still be willing to testify in the trial?
- If a newspaper reports about the loss of sensitive data on a USB drive, what will be the resultant damage to the image of the company involved?

5.5.2 Qualitative risk analysis

Another method of risk analysis is qualitative, and here numbers and monetary values are not assigned to components and losses. Instead, qualitative methods walk through different scenarios of risk possibilities, and rank the seriousness of the threats and the validity of the possible countermeasures. Qualitative analysis techniques that may be used include judgment, best practice, intuition and experience. Examples of qualitative techniques are Delphi, brainstorming, storyboarding, focus groups, surveys, questionnaires, checklists, one-on-one meetings, and interviews. The risk analysis team will determine the best technique for the threats that need to be assessed, bearing in mind the culture of the company and individuals involved with the analysis.

When a team is performing a risk analysis it gathers together personnel who have experience and knowledge of the threats being evaluated. This group is presented with a scenario that describes threats and loss potential, and each member then responds with their gut feeling and experience on the likelihood of the threat and the extent of damage that may result.

Quantitative and qualitative risk analyses each have their own advantages and disadvantages. Management, in consultation with specialists, determine which method should be applied in which particular situation.

5.5.3 SLE, ALE, EF and ARO

SLE stands for **s**ingle **l**oss **e**xpectancy, and ALE for **a**nnualized **l**oss **e**xpectancy. The SLE is an amount that is assigned to a single event that represents the company's potential loss if a specific threat were to take place:

asset value x exposure factor (EF) = SLE

The **e**xposure **f**actor (EF) represents the percentage of loss a realized threat could have on a certain asset. So, for example, if a data warehouse has an asset value of €500,000, it might be estimated that if a fire were to occur, 25% of the warehouse would be damaged (and not more, because of a sprinkler system and other fire controls, proximity of a firehouse, etc.), in which case the SLE would be €125,000,=. This figure is derived to be inserted into the ALE equation:

*SLE x **a**nnualized **r**ate of **o**ccurrence (ARO) = ALE*

The annualized rate of occurrence (ARO) is the value that represents the estimated frequency of a specific threat taking place within a one-year timeframe. The range can be from 0.0 (never) to 1.0 (at least once a year) to greater than one (several times a year) and anywhere in between.

For example, if the probability of a flood taking place in London is once in 100 years, the ARO value is 0.01.

5.6 Countermeasures to mitigate the risk

The risk analysis produces a list of threats and their relative importance. The next step is to analyze each serious threat and to find one or more countermeasures that can reduce this threat. The countermeasures may be aimed at:
- reducing the chance of the event occurring;
- minimizing the consequences;
- a combination of the two.

5.6.1 Categories of countermeasures

How do we define an information security plan? This can be done in various ways and depends on the objectives. Security measures should always be linked to the results of a risk analysis and based on the reliability aspects and characteristics of information.

What do we wish to achieve? This can be divided into six different categories, see figure 5.1:
1. *Preventive* countermeasures are aimed at preventing incidents;
2. *Reductive* countermeasures are aimed at reducing the likelihood that a threat will occur;
3. *Detective* countermeasures are aimed at detecting incidents;
4. *Repressive* countermeasures are aimed at limiting an incident;
5. *Corrective* countermeasures are aimed at recovering from the damage caused by an incident.
6. *Acceptance* of risk is a possibility too. Depending on the level of the risks we can also choose to accept certain risks. A company can invest in insurance, because it decides that the chance of a threat becoming a reality is too low to invest in expensive countermeasures.

5.6.2 Prevention

Prevention makes it impossible for the threat to occur. Examples in IT security are: disconnect Internet connections and internal network connections.

In physical security: closing doors to prevent people entering the building, though this countermeasure is not very practical. There are other preventive measures that are more practical. For example, customers must be able to enter the building, but to prevent unwanted visitors put security zones in place where sensitive information can be kept more safely than in the public zone. Placing sensitive information after office hours in a safe is a second example of a preventive countermeasure. Another example is video surveillance with stickers on the windows informing people they are being monitored.

Change control within quality management systems (QMS) and information technology (IT) systems is a formal process used to ensure that changes to a product or system are introduced in a controlled and coordinated manner. Change control (and ITIL Change Management) is a preventive process to reduce the possibility that unnecessary changes will be introduced to a system without forethought. It can also reduce the possibility of introducing faults into the

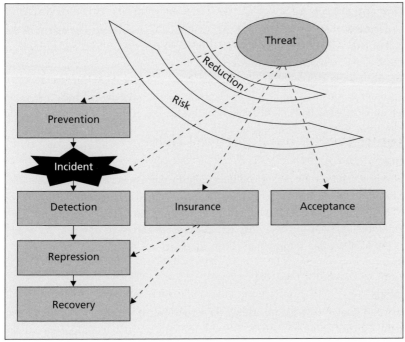

Figure 5.1 Security measures

system or undoing changes made by other users of software. The goals of a change control procedure usually include minimal disruption to services, reduction in back-out activities[16], and cost-effective utilization of resources involved in implementing change.

5.6.3 Detection
When the direct consequences of an incident are not too large, or there is time to minimize the expected damage, detection can be an option. Ensure that each incident can be detected as soon as possible. Simply informing people that Internet use is being monitored will deter many employees from improper Internet browsing activities. An Internet monitoring tool must be in place to detect users' behavior, there is no sense in merely making a preventive announcement about monitoring. Traceability plays a growing role in society and seems to be leading to a shift in the burden of proof.

5.6.4 Repression
When the network monitoring activities of the security officer give an indication that something irregular has happened, action has to be taken. When something actually does go wrong - i.e. when an incident occurs - the thing to do is to minimize the consequences. There is, for example, no point in having fire extinguishers if someone doesn't take the initiative to use them in case of a fire. Repressive measures, such as extinguishing a fire, are aimed at minimizing any damage that may be caused. Making a back-up is also an example of a repressive measure. After all, making a periodic back-up whilst working on a document ensures that the data is not totally lost if an incident occurs. The back-up can be used to restore the last backed-up version of the document, so only a part of the data is lost.

---

16   Back-out: Fail to keep an arrangement or promise

5.6.5 Correction (recovery)

If an incident has occurred, there is always something that must be recovered. The extent of the damage, be it small or large, depends on the repressive measures that were taken. For example, if a colleague were to create a new database that overwrites the previous database, then the extent of the damage depends on the back-up. The older the back-up, the greater the damage done.

A stand-by arrangement is also an example of a corrective measure, whereby fall-back means are put into service on an emergency basis in the event of a disaster. For example, this might include using a different location in order to continue to work.

5.6.6 Insurance

For events that cannot be entirely prevented and for which the consequences are not acceptable, we look for methods that can alleviate the consequence. This is called mitigation. Fire insurance protects us against the financial consequences of a fire. Storing a copy of all important information in a location outside the organization every day ensures that, in the event of a fire, we would at least still have the irreplaceable information. Both measures are not cheap, but are usually regarded as justified.

5.6.7 Acceptance

When all necessary and known risks are identified, the responsible management can decide not to carry out certain security countermeasures. Sometimes costs are not in proportion to the risk posed and the possible damage that might result from this. Sometime there are no suitable countermeasures to mitigate against the threat rather than the risk. The countermeasure reduces the risks.

5.7   Types of threats

Threats can be divided into:
- human threats;
- non-human threats.

To determine threats, information security professionals will often refer to standard lists of threats. These lists are based on best practice and previous experiences. A frequently used list is described in Annex B of ISO 27005, in which the identification and valuation of assets and impact assessment is outlined.

It is necessary to determine which threats are relevant and which are not. Security, after all, requires organizations to spend money and it is not sensible to invest in security against threats that will not actually occur.

We will now look more closely at the types of threats.

5.7.1 Human threats

Intentional human threat. People can intentionally cause damage to information systems for various reasons. We usually think of outsiders such as a hacker who has something against a company and wishes to break into it and cause it damage.

However, what about a company employee who destroys company data after being dismissed, or who, not getting the promotion he or she wanted, takes revenge by destroying data or selling it to the competition.

Waiting for response of the computer because of performance problems can also lead frustrated employees to react excessively on occasions.

Social engineering exploits the lack of security awareness within an organization. Using the right expressions or names of known people and their departments gives the impression of being a colleague. Acting politely and trustworthy may give the 'colleague' the opportunity to obtain company and trade secrets. A social engineer takes advantage of people's weaknesses to realize his objectives. Most people are not aware of social engineering and do not recognize a social engineer. If the helpdesk phones you asking where a particular file is, you should check whether you are actually talking to the helpdesk. Remember, a helpdesk employee will never ask for your password.

Do you ever talk about your work on the train, and are you sure that you do not mention anything confidential? A social engineer works according to a certain pattern. We could write a whole book about social engineering, but will leave it at this for now.

Unintentional threat. People can also cause damage unintentionally. For example, accidentally pressing the delete button and carelessly confirming this with OK. You could also insert a USB stick that has a virus into a machine and spread the virus throughout the network. Alternatively, in panic, you may use a powder extinguisher to put out a small fire and as a result destroy a server. These are typical human responses whereby good security measures are inappropriately applied or subverted.

5.7.2 Non-human threats

There are also non-human events that threaten an organization. These include external influences such as lightning strikes, fire, floods and storms. Much of the damage caused will depend on the location of the equipment in the premises. Is the server room located directly under a flat roof that is susceptible to leaking? Is it situated underground in an area where there is high ground water? Does the server room have windows or is it located in a bunker-style room? All such concerns have an influence on the risks that the organization will face.

We can subdivide human and non-human threats into disruptions to the basic infrastructure such as computer equipment, software or databases, and disruptions to the physical environment such as buildings, paper files, electrical installations, water supplies, heating, ventilation and cooling.

5.8 Types of damage

Damage resulting from the occurrence of the above threats can be classified into two groups:

- direct damage;
- indirect damage.

An example of direct damage is theft. Theft has direct consequences on the business. Another example damage caused by the water from fire extinguishers,

Indirect damage is consequential loss that can occur. An example of indirect damage is being unable to meet a contract due to the IT infrastructure being destroyed by fire, or loss of goodwill by unintentional failure to fulfill contractual obligations.

5.9   Types of risk strategies

We can deal with risks in different ways. The most common strategies are:
• risk bearing (acceptance);
• risk neutral;
• risk avoidance.

Risk bearing, means that certain risks are accepted. This could be because the costs of the security measures exceed the possible damage. But it could also be that the management decides to do nothing even if the costs are not higher than the possible damage. The measures that a risk bearing organization takes in the area of information security are usually of a repressive nature.

Risk neutral means that security measures are taken such that the threats either no longer manifest themselves or, if they do, the resulting damage is minimized. The majority of measures taken in the area of information security by a risk neutral organization are a combination of preventive, detective and repressive measures.

Risk avoidance means that measures are taken so that the threat is neutralized to such an extent that it no longer leads to an incident. Consider, for example, the software patches for an operating system. By patching the OS immediately after the patches are available, you are preventing your system against known technical problems or security issues. Many of the countermeasures within this strategy have a preventive character.

Regardless of the strategy an organization chooses, management has to make a conscious decision and bear the consequences.

5.10   Guidelines for implementing security measures

Implementing security measures thoroughly throughout an organization involves a great deal of work. In many companies, the IT system has developed over the years from a single computer for administration to a large-scale network with many tens or thousands of PCs and dozens, if not hundreds, of servers, inside or outside the office building.

There are guidelines for organizations that help in choosing appropriate measures. A company can, therefore, present a more positive public image by making it clear that it meets these guidelines.

ISO/IEC 20000 is the worldwide standard for IT service management.

Additionally the ISO/IEC 27001:2005 standard deals with the set-up of the information security process. Both standards help in setting up the operational processes in an effective and secure manner.

The ISO/IEC 27002:2005 standard, which is also known as the 'Code of practice for Information Security' contains guidelines for measures in the area of information security. The guidelines in the ISO/IEC 27002:2005 standard deal with the organizational, procedural, physical and logical aspects of information security.

5.11   Springbooks

In this chapter we have covered a great deal about security risks. Imagine you are the new security manager of Springbooks. Up until now Springbooks has only implemented some security measures through the application of best practice in response to security incidents. Now, however, the board has decided that security will be a part of due diligence and you have to point out the approach and the solutions for implementing information security.

Explain what due diligence means for Springbooks and why it has an impact on the duties of the security manager.

Identify what are the most important security risks that Springbooks will have to deal with. You should think in terms of the CIA triangle and risk analysis when considering the potential risks. The Springbooks' order system is centralized in a large computer centre near London. This computer centre is owned by a large IT company. Springbooks has outsourced its IT to this company.

The CISO gets a phone call stating that a vital data cable has been cut by an excavation taking place outside the building. All connections from the computer centre to the Internet have been broken. Springbooks is no longer able to trade via the Internet. The computer company estimates a downtime of at least four hours. Springbooks sells about 12,000 books a day with an average price of € 20. Calculate the loss that the interference to its online business will cause.

6. Business assets and information security incidents

6.1 Introduction

This chapter will explain business assets management and classification, and their role in the information security process.

The information security process is not a one-time event; it is a continuous process. Every organization undergoes constant change, and so the threats, risks and measures also constantly change. Information security must be embedded within the organization and requires constant attention.

It is important that information security is supported by the highest management level within a company, and that this is clearly visible to all staff. Other processes form part of the information security process, such as incident management. What's more, the various tasks involved in the information security can, depending on the size of the organization, be carried out by different people of varying degrees of specialization.

6.2 What are business assets?

Business assets are necessary for an organization. They cost money or have a certain value. Business assets include:

- Information in the form of documents, databases, contracts, system documentation, procedures, manuals, system logs, plans and handbooks;
- Computer programs, such as system programs, user programs and development programs;
- Equipment such as servers, PCs, network components and cables;
- Media in the form of tapes, CD-ROMs, USB-sticks etc.;
- Services (such as buildings, manufacturing equipment, distribution facilities etc.);
- People and their knowledge;
- Non-tangible assets such as the image and reputation of the organization.

Business assets must be classified in order to enable security levels to be set for them. This is the responsibility of the owner. Each asset must have an owner and should be registered in a centrally managed database.

A good and complete registration of business assets is necessary for risk analysis (see chapter 5 for more information on threats and risks). In addition, registration is sometimes necessary for insurance, financial accounting and statutory requirements (for example, the registration of personal data in accordance with legislation for personal data protection). It is best to audit the records of business assets twice per year, and to produce a report of this for the business management.

The information that is recorded about a business asset is:

- the type of business asset;
- owner;
- location;
- format;

- classification;
- value to the business;
- initial cost;
- age;
- estimated replacement cost.

This information may be necessary, for example, after the recovery that follows an incident or disaster.

The owner is the person responsible for a business process, sub-process or business activity and takes care of all the aspects of the business asset including the security, management, production and development.

6.3   Managing business assets

One way of controlling or managing risks is to exert control on changes that pose some sort of risk. This control can be carried out in various ways. There are various models and methods available that help in exerting this control, for example in COBIT™, ISO 20000 and ITIL®. Each of these models or methods has a number of basic elements that help in the control process. The basic elements are:

- Agreements on how to deal with the business assets;
- Agreements (processes) on how changes come about;
- Agreements on who may initiate and execute the changes, and how these changes will be tested.

A pitfall that arises when establishing these, often bureaucratically interpreted, agreements is that they can be elevated to an aim rather than focusing on their significance.

COBIT™ stands for Control Objectives for Information and related Technology and is a framework for setting up and assessing an IT environment in a structured way.

ITIL® stands for Information Technology Infrastructure Library and was developed as a framework of references for setting up management processes within an IT organization. ISO 20000 is the international version of this standard.

6.3.1   Agreements on how to deal with business assets

The purpose of documenting how to deal with business assets is to avoid errors that may arise through incorrect use. Incorrect use can also lead to unnecessary damage. Consider, for example, a simple rule such as not putting paper that contains metal (paper clips, staples) into a paper shredder. The more complex the asset, the more useful it is to set down clear instructions and directions.

6.3.2   The use of the business assets

The use of business assets is subject to certain rules. These rules may be provided in a manual and may, for example, include instructions on how to use mobile equipment when outside the organization. Implementing such rules falls within the scope of organizational measures. See section 10.11 Mobile equipment.

6.4 Classification of information

First of all, we will start with an explanation of a number of terms:

- **Classification** is used to define the different levels of sensitivity into which information may be structured;
- **Grading** is the act of assigning the appropriate classification – such as secret, confidential or public – to specific information. This term is used often within the government;
- **Designation** is a special form of categorizing of information, for example, according to a particular subject matter or organization, or a group of authorized persons;
- The **owner** is the person who is in charge of a business asset. A folder on the network containing information can, for example, have an owner. If someone wishes to have access to that folder, the owner would have to give permission. With laptops, the user is usually registered as the keeper, not the owner. The 'owner' has authority over an asset, the 'keeper' has day-to-day responsibility for it; they should not be the same person.

The *owner* of a business asset assigns an appropriate *grading* in accordance with an agreed list of *classifications*. The classification indicates the form of security that is necessary. This is determined in part by the sensitivity, value, statutory requirements and importance to the organization. The classification is in accordance with the manner in which the business asset is used in the business. The owner of the business asset must ensure it is reclassified if necessary. If business assets within an organization have been classified, only the owner is able to lower this classification (the grading) or give permission to do so. Information, for example, may be classified as confidential up to the moment of publication, but once the information has been made public, the classification is reduced.

If an asset has a grading, it is given a mark or label. This can be placed physically and visibly on the business asset, such as on the computer monitor and on the transmission cables, or inside it, such as is the case with digital documents, databases, records, and messages. A measure for documents could be that the grading must be visible on a certain place on the document. All documents containing classified information must have a copy or version number and page numbering. It must also be clear how many pages the entire document consists of. This is a fairly stringent measure, all the more so as it has to be possible to check each of the measures.

Practically all national governments use a system of hierarchical secrecy which assigns a level of sensitivity to data. From highest to lowest this is usually: Top Secret, Secret, Confidential and Restricted.

A designation can be added to this grading. This designation can indicate a specific group of authorized persons. An example of this is: Police Highly Confidential, Cryptography.

A document with this grading and designation is only intended to be handled by personnel who are authorized to use encryption methods. Within government, people are screened up to the level the classification indicates. Other guidelines are also to be followed, such as access to information on a need to know basis and, of course, the clear desk policy.

The owner determines who has access to the particular designated business assets and who has not. The grading of a business asset also determines how it can be stored physically. For this, business premises are sometimes divided into compartments, with different security requirements for each compartment and increasing levels of security, see: section 7.3 Protection rings.

The use of a grading is very difficult to implement in an organization, as people have to think carefully if they are to apply grading properly. Another possibility is not to assign a grade to non-classified information. This information is public.

If the above is a risk, it can be policy to grade all information as high classification. Thus new assets will be allocated protection rather than assuming they should be 'public'. Careless acquisition of a new asset is thus detected when the people who need to use it can't actually do so!

6.5 Managing information security incidents

Company staff can play an important role in detecting weaknesses in security and noticing security incidents. They are, after all, the first to see the incident:
- Someone has left a confidential document in the printer;
- A file with personal information has disappeared;
- There is an unusual odor in the room where the paper shredder is kept;
- A door that should be locked has been left open;
- A colleague is behaving erratically;
- The PC monitor is showing strange messages.

Staff members must be able to report incidents and these reports need to be acted upon. Usually staff members report such incidents to the helpdesk. The helpdesk employee identifies that this is indeed an information security incident and then carries out the relevant procedure for resolving the incident and reporting it further. If the helpdesk employee is not able to deal with the incident personally (due to insufficient technical knowledge or relevant authority) the incident can be reported to someone with more expertise who may be able to resolve the problem. This is called a *functional (horizontal) escalation*. An incident can also be reported to someone who has more authority and who can make a decision. This is called *hierarchical escalation*. An example of hierarchical (vertical) escalation is notifying one's manager of the suspicious behavior of a colleague.

The purpose of this incident management process is to gain insight into incidents and to learn lessons from them for the future. Such notifications can also initiate another information security process, such as the recovery of a file, a security investigation, or even moving to a stand-by location.

6.5.1 Reporting information security incidents

There are various types of incidents and they occur to various degrees. The ISO/IEC 20000 standard describes how incidents can be managed in the incident management process. But not every incident is a security incident.

> **In practice**
> The IT helpdesk at Springbooks is approached with the question: *"Can you tell me how in Word to get the bold letter function back in the toolbar at the top of my screen"*. This question is recorded as an incident in the helpdesk system, though we cannot call it a security incident, unless there is a 'bold letter button removal virus' of which no one has heard as yet.

The purpose of the incident management process is to ensure that incidents and weaknesses that are related to information systems are known so that appropriate measures can be taken in a timely manner.

Staff, temporary personnel and external users should all be made aware of the procedures for reporting the various types of incidents and weaknesses that can have an influence on the reliability of the information and the security of the business assets.

Staff and users should be required to report all incidents and weaknesses as quickly as possible to the service desk or a contact person. It is, of course, in everyone's interest that the organization responds quickly.

Two matters are of great importance and have to be made clear by the management:
1. Reporting security incidents is primarily a way of learning from them so as to avoid similar incidents from occurring again;
2. Reporting an incident is not intended as a way of punishing the perpetrator of that incident.

However, this is not to say that this may not happen; if an employee was to intentionally sabotage an information system, leak information or cause damage, he or she would have to be reported to the official authorities, e.g. the police.

It is important that people are not afraid of reporting an incident out of fear of the management's response or not wanting to be seen as a telltale.

The process must also ensure that the person who reports an information security incident is informed of the results after it has been dealt with.

Incident reports are also useful when carrying out a (modified) risk analysis. It could be that the measures taken so far are not sufficient to prevent certain incidents.

A standard form on the intranet for reporting such incidents can help to reduce any fear and resistance associated with making these reports. The form can be used not only for giving instructions on any immediate response to the incident that may be necessary, but also for acquiring various details relating to the incident.

An incident report form should, at a minimum, allow the following information to be entered:
- date and time;
- name of the person reporting;
- location (where is the incident?);
- what is the problem? (description of the incident: virus incident, theft, break-in, data loss, etc.);
- what is the effect of the incident?
- how was it discovered?

And, if possible, the following areas should also be covered:
- type of system (desktop, printer, server, mail server, etc.);
- system number / system name (if present);
- who else was informed?

Many other questions are also possible, depending on the type of report. It is important that sufficient information is collected so that the incident can be remedied correctly.

> **In practice**
> - No maintenance is carried out on the equipment;
> - The emergency power supply has not been tested;
> - A colleague loses a laptop computer;
> - A colleague does not adhere to the clear desk policy;
> - A colleague brings along an unauthorized visitor;
>
> - New software is rolled out before being thoroughly tested;
> - A virus has managed to get into the information system;
> - Due to incomplete company data, the profit results are unreliable;
> - The access rights of an employee are not modified after a change of job;
> - Colleagues write their password on note paper that is lying on the PC.

Instructions on what to do in the event of an incident are usually formalized in published procedures. A procedure, after all, describes who does what. Such a procedure should include:
- The analysis of the incident, establishing the cause;
- What steps have to be taken to minimize the consequences of the incident;
- What steps have to be taken in order to determine if corrective measures are necessary to prevent the incident occurring again and, if so, which ones;
- Which parties are to be informed in the event of an incident. This could be those who are affected or those who help to resolve the incident;
- What is reported about the incident and to whom;
- Escalation procedure in case the situation becomes worse or is not resolved in a timely manner.

6.5.2 Reporting weaknesses in the security

When staff, temporary personnel and external users of information systems and services notice that there are (suspected) weaknesses in the system or services, it is important that they report those weaknesses as soon as possible. Only then can incidents be avoided.

When an information security incident is discovered, it is often not immediately clear whether the incident will lead to legal action. There is also the danger of critical evidence being destroyed, either intentionally or unintentionally, before the seriousness of the situation is realized. It is therefore important to firstly report the incident and then ask for advice on the action to take. It is possible that a lawyer or the police need to be involved at an early stage and that evidence will need to be collected.

> **In practice**
> If someone suspects that abusive material is being stored on a colleague's computer, the reporting of the incident has to be done carefully to ensure that no evidence will be removed by this colleague. When starting an investigation one should observe due diligence and due care, observing both the impact of the incident but also legal and regulatory requirements.

6.5.3 Registration of disruptions

In order to be able to analyze a disruption, it is important that the relevant information is collected. This information is often stored in log files. This is the modern version of the traditional logbooks that can still be used today. Imagine there is a power failure and there is no other way of recording the events and actions carried out other than on paper.

In large organizations, disruptions are reported to the service desk (helpdesk). If they are able to, they will resolve the disruption straightaway. If this is not possible, they will pass the relevant information on to a department that can resolve the disruption.

6.5.4 Incident cycle
The incident cycle has the following stages: threat, incident, damage and recovery.
Security measures are aimed at a certain moment in the incident cycle. The measures are intended to prevent incidents (preventive) or reduce the threats (reductive), detect incidents (detective), respond to incidents, stop threats (repressive) and to correct damage (corrective).
The measures are taken in order to ensure the availability, integrity and confidentiality of company information.

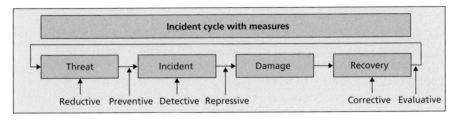

Figure 6.1 Incident cycle with appropriate security measures

6.6 Roles
Depending on the size of the organization, there can be various roles or positions for the various responsibilities in information security. These roles may vary in the title they are given, but they more or less come down to the following:
- The Chief Information Security Officer (CISO) is at the highest management level of the organization and develops the general security strategy for the entire business;
- The Information Security Officer (ISO) develops the information security policy of a business unit based on the company policy and ensures that it is observed;
- The Information Security Manager (ISM) develops the information security policy within the IT organization and ensures that this is observed.

In addition to these roles that are specifically geared to information security, an organization may have an Information Security Policy Officer or a Data Protection Officer.

6.7 Summary

In this chapter you were introduced to incident management. How does an organization deal with security incidents?
It is very important to report incidents; not only in order to be able to solve the incident and to consequently keep the threats and risks for an organization under control, but also in order to learn from them. After all, without knowledge of security incidents, we would not be able to avoid them in the future.

6.8 Case study

Given that Springbooks has shops located throughout the country and across Europe, security incidents are a regular occurrence. Not so long ago, for example, an employee left his laptop on the roof of his car. The laptop was found, but the information it contained was confidential and was not intended for general viewing outside of the company. Within Springbooks USB sticks are also frequently lost. Management believes much more is going on, but is not sure what exactly. The auditing department was unpleasantly surprised when it discovered that there was no security system in place. The director in charge justified this by saying that the personnel knew what they were and were not permitted to do! Under pressure from the auditing department, management appointed a number of people to be in charge of information security.

After a tense round of interviews, you have the honor of becoming the first International Information Security Officer (ISO) within this company. Your primary task is to ensure that:
1. Information security is implemented according to current legislation and regulations;
2. Staff are aware of the benefits and necessity of information security;
3. By the time of the next large company audit, in two years, information security must be well organized and security incidents should be a thing of the past.

What actions will you undertake and how will you carry them out?

7. Physical measures

7.1 Introduction

The previous chapters examined the organization of the information security and discussed risk analysis. A risk analysis determines the level of measures required and where these should be applied. In a separate process this results in a set of security measures that fit with the risk profile determined for the organization.

Some of the measures that were taken as a result of this relate to the physical security of the organization. It all depends on the type of organization. For an organization that has a public function, access to the buildings and the site will be fairly unrestricted. An example of this is a public library. On the other hand, there may be organizations that make products only under very strict security conditions. One example is an organization in the pharmaceutical industry that is subject to very stringent requirements in the area of hygiene and confidentiality regarding the formulae used.

This chapter will take a closer look at physical measures.

Physical measures are often implemented in combination with technical and organizational measures.

7.2 Physical security

Physical security is part of information security because all business assets must also be physically protected . Physical security is older than information security; just think of the protection a castle provides to those inside. Protecting information became important much later in time. Traditionally, physical security is provided by the general and technical services managers who use their own particular methods and techniques to set up the physical security. In many organizations, the coordination between those in charge of physical security and information security is of great importance. We will also examine the various areas of responsibilities that those in charge of information security have to take into account.

The world of physical security employs a combination of organizational, structural and electronic measures. Physical measures need to be planned and coordinated in a coherent way. For example, installing security cameras will only really be effective if structural measures have been taken, and if careful thought has been given to their purpose and placement. What's more, the organization must follow up on anything detected or seen; otherwise installing a camera is totally pointless. The deterrent (preventive) effect of external cameras can be significant, particularly in city-centre locations.

What is often overlooked is that physical measures also apply to temporary (emergency) locations.

7.2.1 Equipment

Physical security includes the protection of equipment through climate control (air conditioning, air humidity), the use of special fire extinguishers and the provision of 'clean' energy. Clean energy refers to the prevention of peaks and troughs (dirty energy) in the power supply and the fact that the power supply is filtered.

7.2.2 Cabling

Cables must be laid in such a way that no interference between the separate cables can occur. Interference is when the network cables pick up the noise and static energy from other power cables that run parallel with them. These effects are often not visible or audible. An example of this effect can be heard when mobile phones cause disturbance in speakers or radios. Cable ducts also have to be protected. Server rooms often use separate power supplies. It is not unusual for a server to have two power supplies, each connected to their own power group.

7.2.3 Storage media

It must be clear to the employees of an organization how they should deal with storage media. Specific measures may apply to certain equipment; consider, for example, the deletion of confidential information on the storage media when a person leaves the organization. Storage media include more than just the obvious forms such as USB sticks and hard disks. Many printers can store information on their own hard disk. Documents can be temporarily stored on printers and can be partially retrieved.

It is also possible to store a great deal of information on mobile equipment, such as telephones, USB sticks, memory cards, organizers, Blackberries, and laptops. It is important that if an employee leaves the company, that they return all their equipment, and that the information contained on them is deleted. There must also be procedures for when such equipment is lost or stolen.

7.3   Protection rings

All business assets represent a certain value, and depending on that value, as well as the threats and risks to these assets, specific measures must be taken. Physical security measures are taken to protect information from fire, theft, vandalism, sabotage, unauthorized access, accidents and natural disasters.

Where does physical security start?

Physical security does not start at the workstation or workplace but begins outside the premises of the business. It must be made impossible for anyone to easily access the company assets that are to be protected. This can be illustrated simply and clearly by thinking in terms of a series of rings:

- Outer ring – area around the premises;
- Building – the access to the premises;
- Working space – the rooms in the premises, aka 'Inner Ring';
- Object – the asset that is to be protected.

7.4   The outer ring

The outer ring that surrounds the business premises can be protected by natural and architectural barriers. Natural barriers can be, for example, thick vegetation or a river. Examples of architectural barriers include fences, barbed wire, and walls. All architectural barriers are subject to strict rules. The outer ring must allow access to authorized persons, so barriers must always employ personal and/or electronic verification. These days there are many types of electronic sensors that are available, but we will not discuss these here.

The area between the outer ring and the business premises (the inner ring) can be used for surveillance by a security guard and for auxiliary services such as, for example, parking, where the parking area is preferably screened off from the building. Such areas must have the appropriate lighting and possibly camera surveillance.

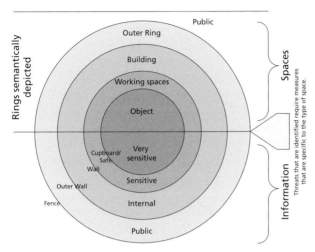

Figure 7.1 Protection rings

7.5 The building

There are situations where there is no outer ring. In these cases architectural measures such as windows, doors and other openings are important. It is, of course, best that appropriate security measures are integrated whilst the premises are being built, as modifying an existing building can be very expensive.

Architectural measures are also subject to strict regulations. There are various ways of making openings in the premises secure; for example the use of break-resistant glass and doors with the correct frame and hinge mechanisms prevent easy break-ins. The measures must be in line with the level of protection required by the organization.

In addition to the traditional locks, of which there are many types, increasing use has been made in recent years of electronic means to control access to buildings. These include card systems and code locks. However, biometric equipment is still not commonly used. Biometrics refers to technologies that measure and analyze human body characteristics, such as fingerprints, eye retinas and irises, voice patterns, facial patterns and hand measurements, for authentication purposes. Biometric characteristics can be divided in two main classes: *physiological* that are related to the shape of the body and *behavioral* which are related to the behavior of a person. In protecting the building, attention must also be given to the roof and walls. Surveillance cameras can again help with this.

7.5.1 Access management

There are various options available to manage the access to business premises:

• electronic access management;
• security guards.

Electronic access management

Many organizations use pass systems with wireless RFID passes. These are currently the most widely used systems, but are the subject of much discussion as they can be 'tapped', copied and mimicked.

In the news

In more than half of the maternity wards in the American state of Ohio, both mother and child are given an RFID tag in the form of a wrist band or ankle band. In this way the wards hope to ensure that babies do not go missing, be abducted or given to the wrong parents. Babies are given an ankle band whilst the mothers are given a wrist band. The HUGs system sounds an alarm if the ankle band breaks or if the RFID tag of the mother does not match that of the child.

Privacy protection organization *Consumers Against Supermarket Privacy Invasion and Numbering* (Caspian) has campaigned against this. They believe that HUGS will make hospitals less vigilant, as hospital workers will rely too much on the technology.

In addition to RFID passes, there are other types of passes that cannot be tapped.

When using access passes, a few complementary organizational measures are recommended:

- Put a photo on the pass. This makes copying a little more difficult. Both the security system and the personnel are then able to check whether the pass belongs to the bearer;
- A pass should only have one owner/user otherwise it is not possible to determine wo accessed the building/room;
- Do not put the company name or logo on the pass, use a neutral design. If someone finds the pass, its purpose must not be obvious;
- Require staff to wear the pass visibly. This should also apply to visitors, so that security and personnel can detect and approach anyone not wearing such a pass. All such passes should also display a human readable expiry date. Ensure that a system is set up whereby people who do not have a pass are escorted to the security staff.

For special rooms, vigorous authentication measures can also be used where, in addition to the access passes, further security measures are taken, such as:

- Something that you know, for example a PIN code;
- Something that you have, for example a pass;
- Something that is part of you (biometrics) such as a fingerprint or an iris scan.

Security guards

The use of security guards is the most expensive physical security measure. This measure can be supplemented by cheaper measures such as sensors and cameras that can be remotely monitored. In this case, there should always be a follow-up procedure if an alarm were to go off.

It is best for the security personnel to also personally verify the access passes of those entering the building. This way it is harder to use fake passes.

7.6 The working space

Each working space may have its own particular function and so would be subject to its own security measures. For example, in a public building such as a town hall we can enter the public areas of the building but the offices are not accessible for everyone.

7.6.1 Intruder detection

In rooms on the ground floor and other special rooms, various types of intruder detection methods can be introduced. This depends on the type of room (size, type of wall, height, contents). The most commonly used method is passive infrared detection. Apparent motion is detected when an infrared (electromagnetic radiation) source with one temperature, such as a human, passes in front of an infrared source with another temperature, such as a wall. Of course, if the intruder detection system sets off an alarm, it requires an immediate response.

7.6.2 Special rooms

It is recommended that an organization sets up special rooms and areas for suppliers to pick up and deliver goods so that they do not have access to the same business assets and information as the company's employees. The restriction of access is a preventive measure. There are a number of other important rooms and associated requirements:
• storage of sensitive materials;
• server room;
• cooling;
• emergency power;
• humidity;
• fire.

Storage of sensitive materials
Separate rooms can be used to store sensitive materials. This can be information, but also medicines or expensive items. These rooms require extra measures to ensure their security. Access to special rooms must be checked, preferably by including these in the access control system of the premises.

Server room
Server rooms and network rooms deserve a separate mention as they have to be approached separately when considering physical security. Server rooms and network rooms contain sensitive equipment that is vulnerable to humidity and warmth, and produce heat themselves. Also, an information system can stop functioning due to a power failure. One of the greatest threats to a server room is fire.

In addition to architectural requirements, server and network rooms also have special access control requirements.

Media such as back-up tapes must not be stored in network rooms. It is best to store the tapes elsewhere, so that the tapes are not damaged in the event of a disaster in the server room. There's nothing worse than discovering after a fire that none of the information can be recovered because the back-ups have also been destroyed.

Cooling

In server rooms, the air has to be cooled and the heat produced by the equipment must be transported away. This air is also dehumidified and filtered. What often happens is that extra equipment is placed in the room without then adjusting the cooling capacity of the room.

In practice

Figure 7.2 Example of air conditioning units

In an organization a cooling installation was placed in the server room many years ago. In the years that followed more equipment was placed in the room, but the cooling capacity of the room was not increased. Eventually the cooling system broke down, causing the temperature to rise. As a result, the servers failed, leaving the business without its central computer system for several days.

Emergency power

Equipment uses power, often a lot of power. In server rooms, it is advisable to use several independent power supplies. A number of other measures are used in addition to this:

- Battery packs or an Uninterruptible Power Supply (UPS) which, in addition to adjusting for fluctuations in the power supply, filters the power and absorbs any peaks;
- Battery packs typically last for just a matter of minutes to a few hours, so it is wise to also have an emergency generator to provide power for any outage that is longer than that which the battery can support. The generator needs to be tested regularly and must be supplied with enough fuel for a sufficiently long period of time. Batteries also need to be replaced every four years or so.

Power failures are a problem not only for computers but also for production companies.

In the news
Brazil Suffers Widespread Blackout
RIO DE JANEIRO (Nov. 11) - Brazil
A widespread power outage plunged as many as 60 million people into darkness for hours, in Rio and Sao Paulo and several other big cities the power went out for more than 2 hours. There was a major problem with a power dam. With no power there was the opportunity for muggers to rob people. The Metro and other transport systems failed.
When companies have not thought about the implications of a major power outage, critical systems will stop and possible damage occurs to data.

Humidity

Any dedicated equipment room (housing printers, networks etc) should be controlled and monitored. These rooms must not contain any moisture. For this reason, the air in these rooms is dehumidified. We must also ensure that no water pipes and central heating equipment have been fitted in these rooms. In early days mainframe computers were water cooled, but even today it is still possible to water-cool equipment, though such solutions must be inspected very carefully. The cooling systems need regular maintenance, and usually use de-mineralised water of which a reserve supply sufficient to refill the system should always be kept on-site.

Fire

See also: section 7.9 on Fire protection.

Fire is one of the biggest threats to computer equipment that a special room, such as a server room or network room, can face. Certain measures are relevant here at all times:

- Smoke alarms to detect the smoke;
- Fire extinguishing equipment. If a fire breaks out, it must be extinguished quickly with the appropriate fire extinguishing equipment;
- No packaging material or supplies/cleaning chemicals should be stored in these rooms. A server room is not a warehouse;
- Back-up tapes should not be stored in the computer room or indeed the building itself;
- Special fire-resistant cabling should be used.

7.7   The object

The 'object' refers to the most sensitive part that has to be protected, the inner ring. Various options are available for storing and protecting sensitive materials:

- cabinets;
- fire resistant cabinets or security cabinets.

Cabinets

A cabinet is the simplest way of storing things. It has to be possible to lock the cabinet, and the key must not be kept nearby. A cabinet is not particularly resistant against fire and can be relatively easily broken into.

Fire-resistant cabinets or security cabinets

A fire-resistant cabinet protects the contents against fire. Fire-resistant cabinets are available in various classes that indicate the degree to which they are fire resistant. Fire-resistant cabinets are not safes but they can also have burglar-resistant properties.

Fire-resistant cabinets are a good means of storing, for example, back-up tapes, paper documents and money. It should be pointed out here that the back-up tapes of a system must not be stored in the same premises as the information system. If the premises were completely destroyed, it is vital that the tapes are still intact.

Fire-resistant cabinets or safes can be cemented in and can sometimes be entire rooms.

Fire-resistant cabinets or safes can have a variety of locks and protection against break-ins.

7.8   Alarms

7.8.1   Sensors

Physical security uses various types of sensors. The most common are:
- Passive infrared detection - these sensors are usually used indoors and detect temperature changes within a certain distance from the sensor;
- Cameras - these sensors record images which can be viewed at a later time. Certain smart software allows automatic checks to be carried out;
- Vibration detection - these sensors detect vibrations;
- Glass break sensors - these sensors detect when a window has been broken;
- Magnetic contacts - these sensors detect when a door or window is opened.

7.8.2   Alarm monitoring

The sensors must be connected to an intruder detection system and should be well monitored. There are some systems that can even automatically contact an emergency center of a third party such as a security firm which is responsible for the monitoring. In any case, whenever an alarm is set off, the cause must be investigated. A logbook should be kept of all alarms.

7.9   Fire protection

Fire protection is a special area within physical security. There are compulsory fire protection requirements that must be met.

Fire is a threat that can always occur. Measures therefore must be taken at all times to protect against it. Fires can start in various ways, such as short circuits, defective boilers, human action, faulty equipment, etc. Fires require the following components: flammable material, oxygen and ignition temperature. This is the 'fire triangle'. A fire can be combated using an extinguishing agent, the purpose of which is to break this fire triangle by elimination the fire's access to oxygen or fuel or by reducing the temperature.

What sort of damage can be caused by fire?
- Damage by burning;
- Damage by heat;
- Damage by smoke;
- Damage by the extinguishing agents used.

7.9.1   Signaling

In order to signal the presence of fire, smoke alarms are usually used and are typically connected to a separate system. It is very important that the smoke alarms are checked regularly.

Organizations should regularly carry out fire and evacuation drills so that everyone is familiar with the sound of the alarm and the evacuation procedures.

7.9.2   Fire extinguishing agents

Fire extinguishing agents are aimed at combating one or more of the three components of fire and, in doing so, putting out the fire. There are different sorts of fires, and therefore also different methods of putting out these fires. Examples of various sorts of fires include: fire caused by electricity, chemical substances that burn or flammable liquids. The various fire extinguishing agents include:

- Inert gases (a gas that suppresses oxygen) such as: carbon dioxide, argon (a type of noble gas), Inergen (brand name) and Argonite (brand name). These are known as flooding systems;
- Foam (water-based, not suitable for electricity);
- Powder (suitable for electricity, but damages metal);
- Water (not suitable for electricity);
- Sand (suitable for oil).

Below we can see the fire extinguishing installation of a server room. Where flooding systems (such as the picture below) are installed special human safety systems are required.

Figure 7.3 Examples of fire extinguishing equipment found in a server room

7.10 Summary

This chapter on physical security covers quite a lot of ground. In essence, you have been introduced to the manner in which we try to protect our property.

We first determine who is allowed to enter our grounds, and decide whether or not to place a fence around the area. If we do, how high does the fence have to be? Do we install cameras inside and outside the building? Is everyone allowed to walk around the building, or do we use access control systems inside the building as well?

As you have read, physical security is by no means just protection against theft. It is also concerned with the cooling of machines. An overheated server will quickly break down, which would then affect the continuity of IT operations. Protecting cables against any form of disruption means a better working environment.

Emergency power equipment ensures that we can continue working if the power were to fail (temporarily).

We have also learnt that only implementing physical security measures is not sufficient to protect the reliability of information. Physical security measures should be implemented together with complementary technical and organizational measures. These will be discussed in the following chapters.

7.11 Springbooks

The data center for Springbooks is too small for their growing IT needs. Springbooks wants to move all of its IT to a new data center that is equipped for the future. The data center must be equipped with all necessary physical measures to ensure that there is minimal damage should a fire break out.

What physical measures would you suggest should be taken to ensure that in the event of a fire minimal damage will occur to the IT systems?

What measures are relevant at all times regarding fire?

8 Technical measures (IT security)

8.1 Introduction

A risk analysis of IT security will result in a set of security measures that fit with the risk profile determined for the organization. Technical measures in automated environments are called IT security measures and are applied in the IT infrastructure. This chapter will examine the security of the IT infrastructure and the protection of data against undesired access through access control, and security measures that can be implemented using cryptographic mechanisms. Since most data is currently processed by or through software applications it is paramount that these applications handle the data as intended by the application owner. The reliability of the information is directly dependent upon the reliability of the software used for information processing. We will also take a closer look at the correct use of an application.

8.2 Computerized information systems

Although information systems are not necessarily computerized, the reality of daily life is that computerized systems are playing an increasingly important role in information processing. As a result, the security of the computerized systems and the associated infrastructure is ever-more important. IT security is the discipline that is focused primarily on the security of the IT infrastructure. This chapter will examine the security measures that can be taken in the area of IT.

8.3 Logical access control

'Logical access control ensures that access to assets is authorized and restricted based on business and security requirements' (ISO definition).

This means that logical access control is also aimed at preventing non-authorized people from gaining logical access to anything that has a value to the organization. In organizations that have strict compliance policies, authorizations are typically granted by the person responsible for the asset, usually a manager. It is also possible that in certain cases individual users can authorize access to assets such as information or applications for other users.

An authorization consists of a set of permissions. Such a permission can be very simple, for example the right to read a certain file or change a record in a database. Permissions can also be very complex, such as the permissions that are needed to make bank payments to suppliers based on invoices. In the latter case a user authorization requires at least the permissions to read invoices from suppliers together with permissions to make bank payments based on the invoices. A number of different concepts are available to implement access control within an automated system. The kind of access control that should be applied to an asset needs to be determined by the asset owner. Once the type of access control is chosen, it needs to be implemented by the system developer or system administrator. The concepts that are described in this chapter are, Mandatory Access Control, Discretionary Access Control, Role Based Access Control and Claim Based Access Control.

8.3.1 Discretionary Access Control (DAC)

With Discretionary Access Control, a data owner and individual users are able to define what access will be allowed to their data regardless of policy, at their own discretion. An example of this is giving others access to one's own home directory. Another example is sending information to persons who do not have access to that information. The major advantage of DAC is that it is very flexible from a user point of view. The downside is that this form of access control is not useful in environments where compliance requirements are very strict. This is especially true if the user who is granting access is not the asset owner.

In order to conform to compliance requirements an organization should be able to prove that information is handled in line with set policies. This should be of concern to the asset owner since he/she can't ensure that the automated system operates according to these policies. As a result, systems working with this flexible form of access control are usually difficult to audit. The main reason for this difficulty is that with Discretionary Access Control each user makes decisions on granting access. In order to check if these decisions are in line with a policy, it should be clear for each user what the grounds were for granting access and to subsequently check these grounds for compliance with the access policy of an organization.

8.3.2 Mandatory Access Control (MAC)

With Mandatory Access Control, permissions are derived from a policy. Owners and users can only permit access to others within the limits of these policy statements. Usually such a policy is centrally managed. A MAC policy contains descriptions of subjects, such as people, systems or applications, and objects such as information, together with other applications or systems. MAC uses attributes such as clearance and classification that are linked to subjects and objects. In a MAC based system access is granted or denied by evaluating if the attributes of the subject requesting access match the requirements of an object.

In a MAC based system individual users are not able to override security policies as is the case in a DAC environment. Typically the MAC policies for an information system are maintained by a system administrator. An example within a corporate environment would be the servers where users can store their files. The directories (the object) to which users (the subject) have access is determined centrally, for instance only those directories for projects that a person is working on. The Mandatory Access Control policy would state that a user or data owner can access a directory if he is working on the related project. It is not possible for this user to change this policy without the support of a system administrator. Within a MAC environment a project member wouldn't be able to give a non-project member access to the project directory.

8.3.3 Role Based Access Control (RBAC)

Role Based Access Control has some similarities with MAC. The main difference is that authorizations aren't based on an evaluation between attributes, here the access decisions are based on the subject's, usually a person's, role. One of the drivers to introduce RBAC is that within an organization there are more users than roles. Since the management of all authorizations for each user costs money, it is possible to save money when the number of users or different authorizations can be reduced.

Take the previous example of a user granted access based on the fact they are working on a project. Within a project there are usually different project members with different roles. Within RBAC a user would be assigned a role within a project and, based on their role, access would be given access to certain parts of a project directory. For instance a project controller would have access to the financial information and deliverables but not to any other project deliverables such as presentations and reports. Conversely, a project member would have no access to the financial information related to the project they are working on. The project leader would have access to all information related to their project. As with MAC, the RBAC access is centrally controlled at the information system level, well outside the direct control of the user. RBAC limits the variation in the number of different authorizations within a system.

8.3.4 Claim Based Access Control (CBAC)

Claims Based Access Control is a relatively new and more flexible form of access control. Within Claims Based Access Control the owner of the information or a system defines a set of claims that he requires before granting access. An example of such a claim is, 'the user works for organization X'. Another example of a claim is, 'the user has the role of project leader'. With this latter claim it is easy to see that Role Based Access control can be implemented on the same basis as CBAC. The advantage of CBAC is that it is more flexible since one is not limited to claims related to a role.

8.3.5 Granting access

Granting access to authorized users involves a number of steps which include identification of the user, authentication of this user and authorizing the user to access an asset. Identification is the first step in the process to granting access. In identification a person presents a token, for example an account number or username. The system then needs to determine whether the token is authentic. To determine the authenticity of, for example, a username, the system checks if the username exists within the system. If the username exists the user is requested to give a password. The systems tests if the password is registered with the given username. If both these tests are valid, a user is authenticated. In this example, authenticating the username is based on its existence in the system and a valid password. From this information it can be derived that a valid user is requesting access. Subsequently the system checks the resources to which access may be granted based on the permissions attached to authenticated user.

> A user checks the catalog of the bookstore online. No user authentication is required at this point since the user isn't doing any transaction that is seen as a risk. Subsequently the user clicks on a book requesting to put it in a shopping cart. When he wants to check out this shopping cart, in order to ship the book to his home address, the bookstore needs to have assurance that the book is paid for before it is shipped.
>
> The system asks the user to provide a client number and password, and based on these the system determines that it is a registered user, and gives the user access to the ordering pages of the online bookstore. In order to complete the order and ship the book, the book needs to be paid before it is shipped. Therefore the system requests the user to provide credit card details. Once the credit card details are checked and the payment is authorized by the credit card company, the book order is completed and the book is shipped to the user.

8.3.6 Security guards at access points

In addition to access control it is important to monitor who has access to what, and whether this authorization is abused. At the online bookstore it has to be ensured that I do not try to gain access to the payment information of other users, for which I am not authorized. Another example is the access that logistics employees have to the corporate payment system. This guarding of access to certain logical areas can be for various reasons, such as restricting the risks of identity theft or the theft of money, as well as meeting certain statutory requirements such as privacy regulations. It may need to be shown that only authorized persons have access to certain information. This clearly shows that granting access is not only a technical matter, but that it is also an organizational concern.

8.4 Security requirements for information systems

From the first moment that a company considers purchasing and developing an information system, it is advisable that security forms part of the project. The main reason for this is that adding security to an information system at a later stage is usually more costly than including it in the initial design. In some cases it isn't even possible to secure a system at a later stage because of fundamental design errors.

Designing secure information systems is not easy, since they usually comprise of operating systems, infrastructure, operational processes, ready-made products, services and applications. The design and implementation of the information system that supports the operational process can be a decisive factor in the way in which security is set up. Adding security at a later stage in one of the elements of an information system can have negative effects on other parts. For instance when a vulnerable network service is changed, it can result in an application not working any more if it was dependent on that specific network service. To avoid such problems as far as possible the security requirements need to be agreed upon and documented before information systems are developed and/or implemented. As information systems are made up of many interrelated and dependent elements it is considerably cheaper to implement, test and maintain security measures during the design phase than during or after the implementation. When security requirements are documented during the risk analysis and specification of requirements for the project, they are justified, agreed upon and documented as part of the total 'business case' for an information system

In order to avoid problems at a later stage, when buying a product, a formal test and purchasing process should be followed. The contract with the supplier must state the requirements that the product's security has to meet. If the security functionality in the product does not meet the requirements, then the resulting risk and the associated security measures will have to be reconsidered; as indeed should the question of whether or not to actually buy the product itself.

8.4.1 Correct processing in applications

Applications (software, computer programs) must work reliably, which means that they have *consistent intended behaviour and results*. A program that causes errors, allows data to be lost, or enables unauthorized persons to make changes or misuse information, could result in a significant risk for an organization. Application systems and applications that have been developed for the user should incorporate suitable protective measures. Such protective measures concern the validation of the data that is entered, the internal processing and the output data. This means that the information has to be entered in such a manner that the data can be checked to see whether it is correct.

One way of implementing controls on internal information processing within an application is to limit the values that data can have within a system and set alarms once these values are reached. Another control possibility is to use the logging of essential functions in the information system. The logs can be checked periodically to ensure, for instance, that parts of the programme are being run in the correct order and by valid users, and can help to detect problems or misuse of an information system.

> Within the online bookstore application a number of tests are integrated to check for suspicious or erroneous orders. One very simple control is that users can only order books that are included in the bookstore's online system. Users are not allowed to order book titles based on free format input. They can search the system using the free format function, but are not allowed to order books with this function. This makes sure that there are no errors in the book titles being ordered as a result of typing errors by the user. A more advanced control is one based on historical order information. Using this information the bookstore manager knows that an average user orders a maximum of 10 books and that usually there are no more than three of the same titles in one order. Orders within the application are always checked for deviations and, as a service, users are contacted to reconfirm those orders that exceed such limits.

8.4.2. Validation of input and output data

Data that is entered into applications should be validated in order to ensure that it is accurate. Business transactions and fixed data can be checked automatically. Validation is an important tool to protect against mistakes and misuse from users, and can take various forms. Where, for example a postal code is used, the format is checked. Another form of validation is to validate within a range, for example a user is not allowed to make transactions greater than €1,200.

In order to simplify the input of data and make it less prone to errors, master tables and terminology lists are often used. These lists, which are built into the application, can prevent more than one word being used for a single term. Using these lists prevent users from making typing mistakes. However, it doesn't automatically prevent users from selecting the wrong item from the list. Consider, for example, an input field for the postal code that always has a fixed format. This applies just as well for sale prices, exchange rates, tax rates and credit limits. It is also important to realize that using predefined lists limits the flexibility of the system. This shouldn't be a problem for well defined processed where all information that needs to be in entered in the system is limited to such a list. When all input cannot be anticipated it is important to have an option to augment the list, either by user discretion or through a moderator.

8.5 Cryptography

To pass the EXIN exam: Information Security Foundation based on ISO/IEC 27002, the candidates need to understand the concepts 'cryptography', 'digital signature' and 'certificate' without technical knowledge about how they work. Sections 8.5, 8.6 and 8.9elaborate on cryptography.

The term cryptography comes from the Greek, and is a combination of the words kryptós which means 'hidden' and gráfo which means 'writing'. Examples of cryptography are as old as the proverbial road to Rome. It was actually used by the Romans to convey military messages. Even if the message were to fall into enemy hands, they would not be able to derive any information from it as the message would appear meaningless. Research into cryptographic algorithms is also referred to as crypto analysis and is used not only to develop algorithms but also to crack the algorithms of enemies. Crypto analysis made particular advances during and after the Second World War.

The main reason to use cryptography is often seen as a means to keep information confidential. It is important to realise that different cryptographic systems exist. Depending on a cryptographic system's capability it can be used for other purposes as well. Other examples of where cryptography is used include data integrity, data authenticity, authentication mechanisms and non-repudiation of information.

The objective of non-repudiation is *to obtain proof of the occurrence or non-occurrence of an event of action* (ISO definition). It is important to note that although the technology is essential to make this possible, the strength of an cryptographic application lies as much in the organizational aspects such as key management.

8.6 Types of cryptographic systems

In order to be able to make use of a cryptographic system, both the sender and recipient must have used the same agreed-upon algorithm. A characteristic of a good cryptographic system is that the algorithm itself is public. Generally speaking, there are three forms of cryptographic algorithms: symmetrical, asymmetrical and one-way encryption.

The Dutchman Auguste Kerckhoffs was a cryptographic expert from the 19th century. He postulated that "the safety of a cryptographic system may not be dependent on the confidentiality of the encryption algorithm but should be based on the secrecy of the key." This means that the algorithm has to be able stand the test of criticism and should be open. The more people that look at it and verify the algorithm before deploying it in applications, the more difficult it will be to penetrate or compromise applications based on the algorithm at a later date. The keys are the secret component of the cryptography.

8.6.1 Symmetrical system

Everyone probably knows some form of symmetrical cryptographic system. A characteristic of such a system is that there is an algorithm and a secret key that the sender and recipient share.

A very well known form of symmetric cryptographic system is the alphabet shift. The key is the number of characters to shift in the alphabet See table 8.1 for a part of the alphabet and its corresponding letters.

Table 8.1 Letters with their corresponding number

A	1	F	6	K	11	P	16	U	21	Z	26
B	2	G	7	L	12	Q	17	V	22		
C	3	H	8	M	13	R	18	W	23		
D	4	I	9	N	14	S	19	X	24		
E	5	J	10	O	15	T	20	Y	25		

In this example we will use the same key with the value of 5 to encrypt and decrypt a word. This means that the letter A (value 1) is replaced by the letter F (value 6). The letter O (value 15) will be replaced with the letter T (value 20). The word 'FLOWER' would be encrypted to the word 'KQTBJW;. Using the same key but then subtracting it from the encrypted (or cipher) text should result in the original (or plain) text FLOWER. In cryptography the text that is to be encrypted is called plain-text. The encrypted version of this plain-text is called cipher-text. The cipher-text can be safely transmitted as long as the key is secret and the algorithm is strong enough. The steps in this example are also shown in figure 8.1

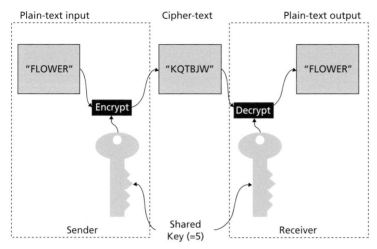

Figure 8.1 Schematic overview of symmetric cryptographic system

In a symmetrical system it is paramount that the key is protected. The same key is used at both by the receiver as well as the sender. Therefore the secret key has to be exchanged prior to the communication from the sender to the receiver. This makes the system vulnerable if the key is not well protected by the sender or receiver, or if the key is intercepted by an attacker when it is sent between the communicating parties. The risk of the key being compromised increases with the more parties that are involved in the exchange of messages using the same key.

8.6.2 Asymmetrical system

An asymmetrical system solves the vulnerability involved in sharing a secret key. The characteristic of an asymmetrical system is that different keys are used for encrypting and for decrypting. The basics for a practical workable system were conceived around 1970 by Ron Rivest, Adi Shamir and Len Adleman and work on the basis of prime numbers and modular arithmetic. An example of modular arithmetic is calculating time with a clock. Imagine a 12 hour clock that indicates 9 o'clock. Adding 8 hours results in a time of 5 o'clock.

The most striking aspect of this algorithm is that it is no longer necessary for the sender and recipient to have the same key. The algorithm works with so-called key pairs. Using this method, the private key is responsible for the encryption and only the public key of this key pair can decrypt the message. What makes this system so special is that the public key can be known to the whole world, as long as the private key is kept secret. Therefore this system is also known as public key cryptography. Within this book we will not go into the technical details on how exactly this algorithm works, it is sufficient to know that the fundamentals of the system are that it uses key pairs, a private and a public key.

The asymmetrical system can be used in two ways. The first way is to sign the message with the private key. Using the public key the recipient can verify whether the message has originated from the owner of the relevant private key. The second way is to encrypt messages intended for a person with their own public key. Only the holder of the private key associated with this public key will be able to decrypt this message. Please note here that the use of the private key is restricted to the holder of the private key, whilst everyone can make use of the public key. In this way asymmetrical algorithms can be employed to guarantee both the integrity and confidentiality of messages. It is evident from this example that one can use the same key pair for both. Keep in mind that the private key is only known to the holder of that key; and since this key doesn't need be shared with anybody else in order to communicate, it isn't vulnerable to the attacks that relate to key exchange as is required in a symmetrical system.

In figure 8.2 the steps in an asymmetrical cryptographic system are shown. The sender uses the receiver's public key to encrypt a message. Since the system doesn't rely on keeping the public key secret, the public key can be sent by the receiver to the sender using the same communication channel as the encrypted message. This makes the key exchange both more secure and much easier than it is in a symmetrical system. The receiver decrypts the message back into the plain-text.

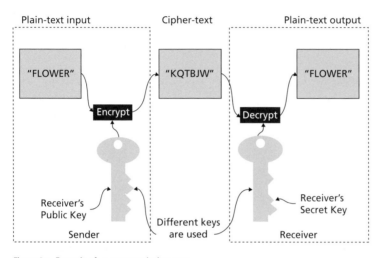

Figure 8.2 Example of an asymmetrical system

Digital signatures are created by using asymmetrical cryptography. A digital signature is a method for confirming whether the digital information was produced or sent by whom it claims to be from - a function comparable with signing paper documents with a written signature. A digital signature generally consists of two algorithms: one to confirm that the information has not been changed by third parties and thus assuring the integrity of the message. The other algorithm is to confirm the identity of the person who has 'signed' the information, thereby assuring non-repudiation.

In Europe, thanks to the Directive 99/93/EG, a digital signature is now regarded as equal to a 'paper' signature. In most cases, it has to be possible to verify this digital signature using an attested certificate which must be made through secure means such as, for example, a smartcard.

8.6.3 Public Key Infrastructure

Although asymmetrical cryptography is also referred to as public key cryptography, it is not the same as Public Key Infrastructure. PKI is based on public key cryptography, and includes much more than just the cryptography. A characteristic of a PKI is that through agreements, procedures and an organization structure, it provides guarantees regarding which person or system belongs to a specific public key. A Public Key Infrastructure is often managed by an independent and trusted authority.

The strength of a PKI depends to a large degree on non-technical aspects. The way a user obtains their private key for instance is a cornerstone in the confidence that other people have in the PKI solution, even if technically they use the same algorithms and key lengths. A PKI where users can get a private key by applying for it by email using, for example, Gmail is inherently less reliable in identifying a person based on his public key than a system where users have to report to a desk and identify themselves by means of a passport before been given a private key.

Non-repudiation is the assurance that someone cannot deny something. Typically, non-repudiation refers to the ability to ensure that a party to a contract or a communication cannot deny the authenticity of their signature on a document or the sending of a message that they originated.

To repudiate means to deny. For many years, authorities have sought to make repudiation impossible in some situations. You might send registered mail, for example, so the recipient cannot deny that a letter was delivered. Similarly, a legal document typically requires witnesses to its signing so that the person who signs cannot deny having done so.

On the Internet, a digital signature is used not only to ensure that a message or document has been electronically signed by the person who purported to sign the document, but also, since a digital signature can only be created by one person, to ensure that a person cannot later deny that they furnished the signature. A PKI is a solution to achieve non-repudiation

ISO defines non-repudiation as *the ability to prove the occurrence of a claimed event or action and its originating entities, in order to resolve disputes about the occurrence or non-occurrence of the event or action and involvement of entities in the event.* .

> The bookstore orders large volumes of books online at a publisher. Because of the high monetary value of these orders, the bookstore and the publisher made arrangements on how to ensure safe orders. Both the bookstore and the publisher have obtained credentials from a registration authority (RA). Within a PKI this RA has the function of checking the credentials against set policies. Once these policies are met, a request is made to a certificate authority (CA) to produce a certificate that states that the public key belongs to the person whose credentials are checked by the RA. Now when the bookstore makes an order at the publisher using a signed message, the publisher can check at the CA whether the certificate is still valid and that the key used to sign the message belongs to the bookstore.

Figure 8.3 gives an overview of the components in a PKI. A user reports to a Registration Authority (RA) and based on credentials (for instance a passport) a request is send by the RA to the Certificate Authority (CA) to issue a certificate. The pair of keys that will be used by the user can be generated in different ways. This is part of the policy used by the PKI. In some PKIs the user can generate these keys, whilst in others a secure facility is used to generate them. The CA issues a certificate signed by themselves that states that the public key belongs to the user to whom the certificate is issued.

In a subsequent action, when the user signs, for instance, a contract with a digital signature, the receiving party can verify if the digital signature really belongs to the user by validating this through a Validation Authority that has access to the Certification Authority.

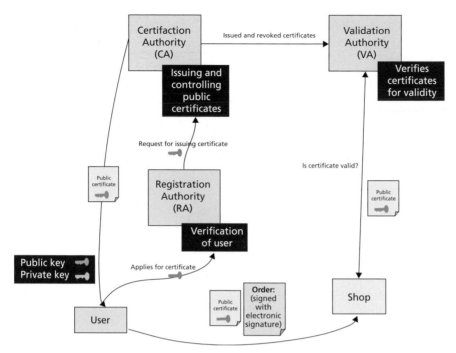

Figure 8.3 Components in a Public Key Infrastructure

8.6.4 One-way encryption

This form of encryption is also called a hash function. A hash function is a non-reversible calculation. The operation of a hash functions can be compared to mixing paint. As soon as two colors of paint mix with one another it is impossible to separate them. When mixing blue and yellow paint, the result is a green paint. It is not possible to obtain the original colours from the mix. It is however possible to mix the two colours again using the same recipe and have the same green colour as a result.

Because of this characteristic this type of algorithm is chiefly used to determine whether data has changed. The message is converted into a numerical value called a hash value. Using a known algorithm, the recipient can check whether the message has the correct hash value; if the two hash values match, the message must be unchanged. Hashes can also be used to confirm that two messages, passwords for example, are the same. When a password is set, the system makes a hash and then stores that hash value rather than the password itself. This way, even a person with high-level access to the system cannot see what the person used for a password. Later, when the person presents the password for authentication, the system again takes a hash of the password and compares it to the hash stored in the system. If the hashes match, the person must have entered the correct password. It is important to understand that this method is used to check the integrity of messages, it does not provide confidentiality.

8.6.5 Key management

The management of the key is an important part of any cryptographic system. Cryptographic keys should be protected against alteration, loss and destruction, since any of these actions could result in an inability to access data. Not that the data is actually lost, but without the appropriate key it is not available in a readable form. Good key management is essential for maintaining data confidentiality. But since losing the cryptographic key is comparable to losing the data, key management is important for the availability of the data. In addition, depending on the use of cryptography in an organization, unauthorized disclosure of the key can have severe implications on the integrity of the data.

What's more, when using cryptography for data confidentiality, secret and personal keys have to be protected against unauthorized disclosure, since this is potentially a breach in information confidentiality. Since the keys are the basis for any cryptographic system, equipment that is being used for generating, storing and archiving keys should be protected physically. A part of key management is the registration of the key pairs and who uses them. When using an asymmetric cryptographic system, pairs of keys are used When using this system to determine message authenticity or non-repudiation, the registration should encompass which pairs have been issued to whom and when. Other topics that should be addressed in key management include how long the keys will be valid for, and what must be done if the keys are compromised.

When using cryptography to protect information stored on equipment it is a major risk to use the same keys for all, or a large part, of the equipment within an organization. If any of these keys become known outside the organization, then that equipment (such as hard disks encrypted in laptops) will have to be provided with new keys, since potentially all data stored on these devices is compromised through the leaking of the one key. This can be a very expensive operation which would have to be carried out very quickly in order to prevent a breach in confidentiality of information.

It is easy to see that the strength of a cryptographic system is directly related to the quality of the key management. This can be illustrated by the following example. Imagine a technically perfect algorithm that cannot be broken, such as a lock that is burglar proof. It is a piece of cake for a burglar to open this lock if he has access to the key. Protecting the key from theft, duplication or destruction is essential for the lock to operate in accordance with its requirements of keeping unauthorized people out and letting authorized people open the door.

8.7   Security of system files

In order to secure a system, all aspects of that system have to be taken into account. This means that not only should the information stored in the system be protected but also essential information about the system itself. Some of the system files are described below.

8.7.1   Access management for program source codes

System files lie at the heart of the computerization of an organization. If the source code of these files falls into the hands of someone with malicious intent, it is possible for that person to gain access to confidential information. One way to achieve this is by modifying the source code before it is actually implemented in the system. The intention is that once the source code is used, the attacker is then able to manipulate the information in the system without having to use a valid user account. These source code files must therefore be treated with the utmost care. Access to the source code of programs must be restricted to only those who have a genuine need for this access.

8.7.2   Security of test data

It is important that equipment and program test data be carefully chosen, protected and managed. Real data, which could contain sensitive information such as personal details, must not be used for testing. Test systems must only use fictitious data. There are number of real life examples where using real life data for system testing has led to unwanted situations.

> The use of real life data for the training and testing of a new system for a government organization mistakenly resulted in people receiving a letter stating that they were deceased. The test data got mixed up with real life data in the production system, leading to a major embarrassment for the local government.
>
> For testing purposes real life data was given to a system tester. The security protocols and measures used by the system tester were less strict than for the real life environment. The tester stored the data on his laptop which was subsequently lost due to a theft. Ironically the real life data was not strictly necessary to complete these tests, but it was more convenient since no extra datasets needed to be generated.

8.7.3 Security in development and support processes

Managers who are responsible for application systems are responsible for both the security of the project environment in which the applications are developed and the environment in which the applications are supported. They also determine whether proposed changes could jeopardize this security. For instance, they need to determine if the system developer has security measures in place that comply with the requirements within their own organization. Assurance about these security measures can, for example, be obtained by auditing the system developer through a third party.

8.8 Information leaks

It is possible for information to leak out through hidden communication channels. However, it would be unusual for the average employee to be aware of the presence of such a communication channel. Secret communication channels are channels that are not intended for processing information, but nonetheless can exist in a system or network. It is difficult, if not impossible, to prevent all possible secret communication channels.

The use of such channels is a common feature of trojans (see section 10.6.1 on Malware). It is possible that the supplier of a bespoke program can leave a secret access method in order to carry out maintenance on the application, without informing the buyer of this. This is referred to as a maintenance door or a backdoor and is a practice not normally appreciated by customers! If the bespoke application is used for processing highly confidential information, then an independent bureau can be contracted to inspect the source code of the application for such secret communication channels.

One example of information leakage is the application of steganography. This technology makes it possible to hide text messages in ordinary pictures such as a photograph. For a user it is impossible to see the hidden message by looking at the picture. A programme is needed to obtain the text information stored in the picture.

8.8.1 Outsourcing program development

When the development of computer programs is outsourced, it is important that this development is supervised and controlled by the commissioning organization. Who becomes the owner of the source code? If possible, the client must have the intellectual property rights. The quality and precision of the work that has been carried out can be determined through certification by an independent body. The importance of this is highlighted when you consider for a moment the discussion above regarding the monitoring of the hidden communication channels.

8.9 Cryptography policy

As has already been explained, cryptography is a measure that an organization can employ if, for example, confidential data is involved. The use of cryptography has to be carefully considered and defined in a policy document. This policy document is the basis for determining how to apply cryptography within the organization's information systems. This document should contain at least the following information:

- What does the organization use the cryptography for; one particular aspect to consider before using cryptography are the legal limitations for exchanging encrypted information with organizations or departments in other countries. This is important since in some cases it is not allowed to use certain types of cryptography or carry cryptographic software across national borders.
- What types of cryptography does the organization use, and in which applications; this is important to limit any problems that come with incompatible applications or cryptographic algorithms. By having a corporate policy and controlling its implementation these incompatibility problems could be kept to a minimum.
- Control and key management of keys; the basis of every cryptographic system are the keys. Usually the algorithms of a cryptographic system are public. The strength of the system is based on the strength of the keys and the ability of the organization to keep these keys from falling in the wrong hands. It is, therefore, paramount for an organization to have clear and strict policies on how to manage these keys.
- Back-up; when making a back-up of encrypted data it is important to determine how the original data can be accessed when required. This is especially important when the key is lost or compromised, which means that unauthorized users have gained access to the key.
- Control; this describes the way the application of cryptographic material is handled by the organization and what measures are in place to limit misuse. Such misuse can include staff wilfully encrypting company data without authority, leaving the company without access to the information.

8.10 Summary

Access to buildings is controlled, as is the access to the network infrastructure. How do we deal with the access rights provided to staff in the IT environment? The rights given to one member of staff can differ from those given to another. How do we determine who is allowed to do what? When that has all been determined, it is then time to distribute the available information to the employees who are permitted access to the particular systems. This is done through access control.

The protection of information against access by unauthorized persons, or the integrity of information, can be achieved by using cryptography. You have been introduced to cryptography and now understand the difference between symmetrical and asymmetrical cryptography and PKI solutions.

8.11 Case study

The bookstore has plans to greatly expand the IT environment. The management board has decided that it is necessary to replace all IT facilities with new equipment. In line with the overall policies, an open source approach is being considered. In order to maintain reliability it is important that all the new hardware is provided with good support. The current computer program that was specifically designed for the bookstore is no longer adequate. The IT department is now going to develop new programs that can be used flexibly on various operating systems (OS). This development may be outsourced.

This bookstore employs large numbers of staff who work in a limited number of areas. There are differences in authorization levels. Only a small number of staff have access to strategic information such as the annual figures and the financial administration. These staff do not, however, have access to customer data, again showing the many separate levels of authorization. All stored data must, of course, be protected against unauthorized access. What's more, the exchange of certain sensitive data with external parties must be encrypted.

It is important that the new system has the means to ensure that only the correct information may be entered. Entries, depending on the amount, are subject to various controls. Very large amounts are checked by more than just one person.

You are given the task of setting up a study into the security of the new network and computer systems that are to be purchased. What are the considerations to be taken into account when you have to decide upon the type of hardware? Explain your decision. What are the requirements for the operating system?

How will you arrange the authorization structure? What techniques will you use to determine the various levels?

Will you choose to have your company carry out the software development or will you use an external company? Give the advantages and disadvantages of both options and indicate the possible pitfalls for the bookstore.

In this case, there are many other considerations that have to be taken into account. Describe these considerations and explain your choices.

9. Organizational measures

9.1 Introduction

In the previous chapters, we have taken a close look at the physical security of the work environment and the technical security of the IT infrastructure.

This chapter will examine various organizational measures. Organizational security measures are often inextricably linked with technical measures. Where relevant, we will refer to the technical measures that are necessary in order to be able to carry out or enforce these organizational measures.

We will, for example, take a closer look at (security) policy, the PDCA cycle and the components of ISO/IEC 27001 and 27002, an important international standard for information security. We will also discuss the information security process and the way in which information security can be propagated in the organization.

How do we deal with disasters? What exactly are disasters and how do we prepare for them?

If a disaster were to occur, what procedure will be followed in order to ensure the security of people and other assets, and to get back into operation as soon as possible?

We will also examine communication and operational processes, test procedures and the management of the IT environment by an external provider.

9.2 Security policy

9.2.1 Information security policy

By establishing a policy for the security of information, management provides direction and support to the organization. This policy must be written in accordance with the business requirements as well as the relevant legislation and regulations.

The information security policy should be approved by the management board, and published to all staff and all relevant external parties, such as customers and suppliers.

In practice, the latter is usually distributed as a summarized version of the policy outlining the main points. This can be in the form of a flyer issued to all staff and included as part of the induction for new personnel. The complete version can be published on the intranet of the company or in some other location that is easily accessible to all staff. However, only publishing the policy on the Intranet is not a guarantee that it will be read by the employees, there must be a well balanced awareness program to reach all employees.

In the news

At Virgin Media, the entertainment branch of Richard Branson's Virgin Group, a CD containing the details of 3,000 customers has been lost. The unencrypted disk contains the bank details, names and addresses of the 3,000 customers who have arranged memberships at various shops since January. The data was placed on a CD in violation of company policy.

9.2.2 Hierarchy

It is common for a policy document to have a hierarchical structure.

Various policy documents are developed, with the high-level corporate security policy acting as the basis. They must always conform to the corporate policy and provide more detailed guidelines to a specific area. An example of this is a policy document on the use of encryption.

The following items may then be written, with the policy documents forming the basis:

- **Regulations**. A regulation is more detailed than a policy document, Regulations are usually considered mandatory and failure to observe them may lead to disciplinary procedures;
- **Procedures** describe in detail how particular measures must be carried out, and can sometimes include the work instructions, for example a clear desk policy. In order to ensure that sensitive materials cannot be easily removed, a clear desk policy is necessary. No information should be left unattended on a desk, and after working hours all information must be stored in something that can be locked;

In practice

Within the general encryption policy of Springbooks there is a procedure on how to deal with a particular means of encryption. This is, therefore, compulsory. The procedure explains to the user how to handle the encryption software and the key itself.

A procedure can also define how the system manager is to install the encryption software. These instructions are very detailed, such as what boxes need to be checked, the number of characters a password requires and for how long the password remains valid.

- **Guidelines**, as the term suggests, provide guidance. They describe which aspects have to be examined with particular security aspects. Guidelines are not compulsory, but are advisory in nature;
- **Standards** can comprise, for example, the standard set-up of particular platforms.

In practice

A Springbooks guideline provides advice on the requirements that a classification policy has to meet. The staff responsible are then free to choose the way in which they will carry out the classification policy for the organization.

An important example of a standard is ISO/IEC 27001:2005. This is a standard for setting up information security in the organization. Part I, ISO/IEC 27001, describes the management system (Information Security Management System, ISMS). Part II, ISO/IEC 27002:2005, which is also called the Code for Information Security, develops this management system through practical guidelines. An organization can have itself certified for ISO/IEC 27001:2005 and consequently show suppliers and customers that it meets the quality requirements for information security. The Code for Information Security is suitable for all organizations, small or large, government or businesses.

9.2.3 Evaluating the information security policy

The information security policy is one thing, implementing it in the organization and checking whether it is being adhered to, is another.

Many organizations work with the PDCA cycle (see figure 9.1).

The information security policy is the main document. The information security policy includes policy documents, procedures and guidelines that are aimed at a certain aspect of information security and which provide detailed expectations. These documents are an important part of the Information Security Management System (ISMS).

9.2.4 PDCA model

The PDCA model, also called Deming's quality circle, is used as a basis for determining, implementing, monitoring, controlling and maintaining the Information Security Management System (ISMS).

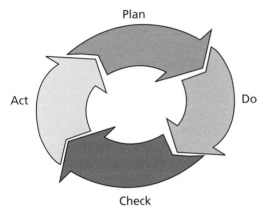

Figure 9.1 PDCA model linked to the ISMS processes

Plan (design the ISMS)

In the design phase, an information security policy is developed and documented. Here the information security objectives, the relevant processes and procedures are defined; these ensure that the risks are managed. These objectives must, of course, support the business objectives of the organization.

The security measures can be adopted on the basis of a risk analysis and a cost/benefit analysis. There are other methods, but we will not go into them here.

The Plan phase applies not only to the main policy but also to all supporting policy documents and underlying regulations.

Do (implement the ISMS)

In this phase, the information security policy and the underlying procedures and measures are implemented. Responsibilities are allocated to each information system and/or process.

Check (monitor and check the ISMS)

In this phase, controls are carried out using self-assessment (internal auditing) and, where possible, measurements are undertaken to see whether the information security policy is being correctly executed. A report on this is issued to the management responsible and the Chief Information Security Officer (CISO).

Act (maintain and adjust the ISMS)

In this final phase, corrections are carried out and preventive measures are taken, based on the results of the internal audit. The ISMS is updated in the light of any particular findings.

The PDCA cycle is a continual cycle. This is described in an ISMS manual.

9.2.5 Setting up ISMS

The organization formulates a framework for the control of its ISMS. This framework provides a logical classification of all the matters relating to information security by arranging them into domains.

A domain is a group of subjects that are logically connected to one another. Domains form the basis to the ISMS framework. These domains sometimes have their own policy documents, procedures and work instructions.

The ISMS comprises at least the eleven domains as identified in the ISO/IEC 27002 standard. These are in line with the processes for IT Service Management as described in the ISO/IEC 20000 standard.

9.2.6 The eleven domains in the ISO/IEC 27002

ISO 27002 defines the following eleven domains for IT Security:
1.   A.5   Security policy;
2.   A.6   Organization of information security;
3.   A.7   Management of assets;
4.   A.8   Security of personnel;
5.   A.9   Physical security and security of the environment;
6.   A.10 Management of communication and operating processes;
7.   A.11 Access security;
8.   A.12 Acquiring, developing and maintaining information systems;
9.   A.13 Management of information security incidents;
10. A.14 Business continuity management;
11. A.15 Compliance.

It should be noted that the domains listed above start from A.5 as these numbers correspond to the chapters of the ISO/IEC 27002 standard. The first four chapters of the ISO 27002 document give an introduction to these eleven domains.
Each domain is divided into a number of sub-domains. For example, access security comprises both physical access and logical access.
A domain is described in a policy objective and is worked out in further detail in underlying guidelines, procedures and aids.

9.2.7 Monitoring the information security policy

The information security policy is regularly assessed and, if necessary, modified. The permission of the management board is required for any changes to the policy.

9.2.8 The information security process

Without effective security of information, it is likely that incidents will occur and the organization will face increased risks which just might result in it going out of business. If it is lucky the organization can carry on its usual business. Everyone in the organization must accept this and the management board and management have to act as examples. Only when they themselves support their own policy, will the staff take information security seriously and so work to comply with the measures.

Information security is a process in which many people are involved. The process needs to be controlled effectively. If there is no responsibility or management, then information security will not be effective. The manner in which information security is managed depends on the size and the nature of the organization. In small organizations, information security can be just one of the responsibilities of several people. A self-employed person without any employees is responsible for all aspects of information technology, including security. In contrast, in large organizations, there will be personnel whose sole responsibility is a particular aspect of information security.

In the information security process, periodic consultation needs to take place between all those with primary responsibility. In addition to the information security officers, these can also be personnel who are responsible for implementing certain measures. Ideally these should be staff who work in the Human Resources, Information, Finance, Accounting or Estate departments.

9.3 Personnel
See also: 'Segregation of duties' in section 10.3.

Personnel can also be regarded as business assets. People and their knowledge and skills are valuable assets, and measures are necessary to protect this value.

All personnel are responsible for information security. This responsibility must be made clear in the employment contract. The staff manual should contain a code of conduct and the sanctions that are imposed in the event of non-compliance and if incidents arise as a result. The code of conduct may state, for example, that private emails are not permitted. The manager is responsible for the correct job descriptions and is, therefore, also responsible for the various aspects related to dealing with information in the various positions.

When a person applies for a job which involves working with sensitive information, references, identity and diplomas must all be checked. In some countries it is possible to get a certificate of good practice. If a person has committed a criminal offence, this can be brought to light by making it compulsory to fill in a 'certificate of good character'. These certificates can be issued by the Department of Justice or some other organization. Background checks may be arranged through the local law enforcement office and should have a scope beyond just the local area. For example, a check for criminal offenses in the U.S. should be run across all 50 states not just in the local County or State.

The organization must have rigorous procedures for when personnel leave and enter employment, or when they change jobs within the organization. It must not be forgotten to change or remove rights, and to collect equipment and passes. Access rights must be controlled regularly.

9.3.1 Screening and Non Disclosure Agreement
For a position involving confidentiality, this confidentiality may have to be observed even after the employment ends. The manager is responsible for documenting special rules for specific positions. In every case, all personnel with a position that involves confidentiality must sign a Non Disclosure Agreement (NDA). It is also usually the case that these personnel have to submit a certificate of good character or agree to a background check.

They may also have to undergo a screening or security examination. How in-depth this screening is, depends on the level of confidentiality associated with the position in question.

Take, for example, security guards, managers and financial staff. Screening is very expensive. The government has organizations that conduct such screening. Businesses can sometimes use such organizations if they carry out work commissioned by the government. However, there are also private organizations that carry out these screenings.

9.3.2 Contractors

The security requirements that apply to the personnel of an organization should also apply to any staff the organization may hire on a temporary basis. The written agreements with the supplier of such staff, such as a recruitment agency, must include sanctions in the event of violations.

9.3.3 Personnel files

Personnel data and personnel files must be handled confidentially and be securely stored. It should also be documented who is allowed to have access to these personnel files.

A personnel file contains information such as the job profile, the employment contract and various signed declarations. A code of conduct for computer use is an example of such a declaration. Other examples include a code of conduct for email use, declarations of understanding and intention to observe legislation (for example in the area of data protection and computer criminality) as well as a Non Disclosure Agreement.

9.3.4 Security awareness

One of the most effective measures for information security is that personnel have to attend a security awareness course when entering employment. This course can be part of their induction training.

In order to support information security awareness, various means can be used: flyers, booklets, messages on computer screens, mouse pads, newsletters, videos and posters.

Large organizations often arrange separate security awareness courses for people such as system managers, developers, users and security personnel. Other groups may also benefit from a course that is specific to their own particular work. These courses and campaigns focus particularly on the company rules relating to information security and the anticipated threats.

Security documentation and information must be available to everyone in the organization. Different documentation is often produced for different target groups (users, managers, developers, etc.). The documentation needs to be revised on a periodic basis, but also when there have been changes or when any new threats appear.

Staff must be made aware of the importance of not allowing company information to get out in the open. Everyday social activities and contacts such as birthdays, clubs, meetings with friends and, in particular, casual acquaintances, form a risk. Information tends to be more easily shared in a relaxed atmosphere, which may then lead to it getting into the wrong hands.

Social engineering is an example of a conscious attempt to extract confidential information from an unwitting victim. For example, someone may try to gain the confidence of an employee by pretending to be a colleague or a supplier, but is really trying to acquire confidential information. In a large organization where not everyone knows one another, there is a good chance of success. The social engineer takes advantage of people's weaknesses. When, for example, we hear someone speak using the correct jargon, we assume that he is part of the organization. Of course, the social engineer may have simply heard these terms in the café.

> **In the news**
> Around Christmas time, when many people buy their (books) gifts on the internet store of
> Springbooks, thousands of customers received an email that was infected with malware.
> The email contained the logo of Springbooks with the invitation to click a hyperlink with a
> hidden IP address. In so doing computers were infected with a trojan, allowing the system to
> be included in a network of infected PCs. This so-called 'botnet' can be remotely controlled
> by cyber criminals and subsequently used to commit crimes. One example is to establish
> fraudulent bank websites that mimic the bank's real website.
> Earlier during Christmas and New Year, a batch of infected emails were sent. The Storm
> Worm is one of the most stubborn threats in the history of the Internet.

9.3.5 Access

For large organizations where not everyone knows one another, a good physical access control
system is of even greater importance. An example of this is a system whereby both staff and
visitors have to wear clearly visible passes.

All visitors have to be registered on arrival and departure. All access is recorded, visitors check-
in and out at reception, and write down their arrival and departure time. An employee who is
expecting a visitor can also check-in the visitor and escort the person around the building up to
the moment of their departure.

9.4 Business continuity management

One cannot be prepared for everything. Floods such as those of Spring 2007 in England and
the Autumn floods in Bangladesh in 2007 caused great losses to the countries' economies. There
was the enormous damage caused by hurricane Katrina in New Orleans. Terrorist attacks in
New York, London and Madrid, as well as simple power failures lasting several hours, can have
considerable consequences for the availability of people and systems within a company.

Each year, companies all over the world are hit by disasters that have a huge impact on the
availability of their systems. Only a small percentage of these companies are adequately prepared
for these eventualities. The majority of companies affected by such huge disasters are likely not to
survive them. The companies that do survive this sort of disaster typically have carefully thought
through the possibility of such disasters and the likely outcomes in advance and have documented
and followed the necessary measures and procedures to protect themselves. However, if no plans
exist it does not mean that the company cannot survive, this depends on the business and other
factors.

An organization is dependent upon assets, personnel and tasks that have to be carried out on a
daily basis in order to remain healthy and profitable. Most organizations have a complex network
of suppliers and assets that are dependent upon one another in order to be able to function.
There are communication channels such as telephone and network connections, and there are
buildings in which work is carried out. The buildings have to be in optimum condition in order
to ensure that the work is not only pleasurable but also carried out efficiently.

If a link in the chain of dependencies fails, this can lead to problems. The more links that fail, the greater the problem. And the longer certain components in the chain are out of action, the greater the effect this has on the organization, and the longer it will take to restart normal operations.

Thinking in advance about the continuity of the work processes is essential for an organization. It does not matter whether this is a complex production process or a relatively simple process such as the processing of residents who have moved to a new house. For both the personnel and the customer, it is important that each component, big or small, of the process works smoothly, and continues to do so in the event of difficulties.

The purpose of Business Continuity Management (BCM) is to prevent business activities from being interrupted, protect critical processes against the consequences of far-reaching disruptions in information systems and allow for speedy recovery.

In the management process of business continuity, the business processes that are critical to the operation of the organization must be identified. In addition to other measures that ensure the continuity, the loss of information that could arise as a result of a natural disaster, an attack, fire or power failure, must be avoided. The consequences of disasters, security incidents and the failure of services are assessed in a Business Impact Analysis (BIA). The continuity plan describes how information required by the critical business processes can be quickly made available.

In information security, continuity management is usually split into two separate, but closely related, components:
- **Business Continuity Planning (BCP)** in which the continuity of the business processes is guaranteed;
- **Disaster Recovery Planning (DRP)** whereby the recovery after a disaster is organized.

Business continuity management is described in the BS 25999, which is a British standard comparable with an ISO/IEC standard.
ISO/IEC 27002 includes some BCM measures, but these are primarily aimed at the information component, while BS 25999 is applied integrally throughout an organization.

9.4.1 Continuity

Continuity concerns the availability of information systems the moment that they are required. Various requirements can be imposed upon this availability. Do you have a telephone exchange where fifty staff are on the telephone twenty-four hours a day? Then you would undoubtedly have different availability requirements compared to a company with only one person on the telephone who receives a telephone call only once every hour.

For a city council, the availability of the municipal database is of great importance. If this were no longer available, then large numbers of staff would not be able to carry out their work. However, if this system were not available to the council at night, this would pose little or no problem.

We can see here that, depending on the organization, the field of work and even the division within an organization, availability requirements can differ dramatically.

9.4.2 What are disasters?

We will now take a closer look at what we mean by disasters. On the face of it, a disaster sounds quite threatening. But nothing is further from the truth. In this context, the failure of a simple system could already be regarded as a disaster. A disaster does not necessarily have to be a flood or a terrorist attack. The failure of the system upon which you depend so much for your daily work, through a technical problem, is also a disaster.

In practice
A simple network card in the mail server that becomes defective can be an utter disaster. These days, staff would not be able to carry out their work properly if deprived of their emails.

How does your company respond to a disaster?

The consequences that a disaster may have on a business depend on the nature of the disaster. If the work has been disrupted due to a failure of a system or the complete network on which the office IT operates, then a telephone call to a service desk or helpdesk is often enough to get the necessary activities back and running. Similarly, if the health of an employee is being threatened, then a telephone call to the in-house emergency service or national emergency number would be the correct action.

In all cases, human life has priority over software and equipment. The evacuation activities have to be set in action first, only then should attention be given to the business processes, starting with the most crucial to the business.

It is important therefore, that clear and effective procedures are in place to define which actions have to be taken, for example:

• You know that, in the event of an information system failing, you have to contact the helpdesk;
• You know where the emergency exits are in the building;
• You know who to phone in the event of a fire, the spontaneous setting-off of the sprinkler system or a bomb alert.

The helpdesk or in-house emergency service worker must know what to do for each type of alert. They will have a priority list which documents who and what has to be helped and when, as well as which organizations they have to contact for each different alert.

The training of in-house emergency service workers is very important. In-house emergency service workers are normal personnel who have decided to take on these additional duties. Ensure that there are in-house emergency service workers throughout the entire organization.

Bomb alert

A bomb alert is obviously a very serious risk to an organization. They are not a normal occurrence in most countries, but if it happens the effect is a disaster and people may well be killed. It is good to see that people have become more aware of suspicious packages. It is therefore strongly advisable to have procedures in place for this threat. The bomb alert procedure must clearly describe what to do in the event of someone raising an alarm. Suspicious items can enter any company. Personnel must know what is not normal and be able to identity suspicious items. Attention should be given to this during the security awareness campaign.

9.4.3 Disaster Recovery Planning (DRP)

What is the difference between Business Continuity Planning and Disaster Recovery Planning? The purpose of DRP is to minimize the consequences of a disaster and to take the necessary measures to ensure that the staff, business assets and business processes are available again within an acceptable time. This is different to BCP, in which methods and procedures are also arranged for failures that last a longer period of time.

A DRP is aimed at recovery immediately after a disaster. The DRP is put into action when the disaster is still ongoing. Work is focused on determining the damage and getting the systems running again. A BCP goes further and has a wider focus. BCP arranges an alternative location where the work can be carried out while the original location is rebuilt. In BCP, everything is focused on keeping the company running, even if only partially, from the moment the disaster occurs up to when the company has fully recovered.

In other words:

- DRP: there is now a disaster and what do I have to do to get back into production;
- BCP: we have had a disaster and what do I have to do to get the situation back to how it was before the disaster.

In practice

An employee of Springbooks uses an *intranet* version of the telephone directory. This suddenly fails so she informs the helpdesk of this. The employee can however continue her work by simply using the *Internet* version of the telephone directory.

Such a message to the helpdesk will not receive high priority.

A Springbooks IT employee is working on recovering the intranet telephone directory. A message comes in that an important system has failed, resulting in the production process coming to a standstill.

Everyone understands that the continuity of such a system will receive higher priority than the recovery of a system for which there is an alternative.

When developing a BCP and/or DRP, a variety of solutions can be considered for getting the business processes running again. If it is decided that, in the event of a disaster, the business processes and systems must be made available as soon as possible, the best option is to develop plans and procedures for a stand-by arrangement. Such arrangements must be tested regularly. The plan also needs to include how the stand-by arrangement, once activated, will be withdrawn; it must be clear under what conditions normal operations may be resumed. It is necessary to estimate the maximum allowable downtime and recovery time for systems and to determine which systems are needed for the organization to continue business.

Alternative workplaces

A large, well-known Dutch bank has, through an inventive use of many different locations, ensured that its staff would be able to carry on working in the event of a disaster. Certain key players in the organization have been assigned alternative workplaces in other branches. If something were to happen at the permanent workplace of these key players, he or she would travel a few kilometers to the alternative workplace. The employee who works at this alternative workplace is aware of the arrangement, and will make room for this key player if necessary.

> **In practice**
> Springbooks has set up a hot site approximately 20 kilometers from the main branch. The Internet bookstore is highly dependent on the computer centre. A failure of this central operational centre could result in a loss of tens of millions of Euros. The costs of this hot site are far less than the costs involved if the system were to fail for some time.

Redundant site

A good alternative for a business with many locations but only a single central computing centre is a redundant site. The redundant site contains a copy of the computing centre. All the data that enters the main computing centre is also entered into the system of the redundant site. Should one of these two locations experience a failure, the other location will automatically take over. When this is done smoothly, the user will not notice a thing.

Hot site on demand

Another solution is a mobile hot site. This is one or more trucks that contain all the equipment necessary to function as a temporary computing centre. In the event of a disaster the trucks are driven in a short time, typically a few hours, to a pre-defined location and the equipment connected up. The possibilities are limited, but it is one way of getting the most crucial processes operational again as soon as possible.

Testing the BCP

These various solutions, varying from cheap to expensive, all sound very effective. A good BCP/DRP team will consider all the eventualities, discuss everything numerous times and eventually gain the approval of senior management. The plan is then published and all managers receive a copy. But then the copies go into a cabinet or drawer. After all, disasters only happen to other people, not us. Don't they?

Well, that is why it is best to test these plans regularly, and to evaluate and modify them when necessary. Organizations change, therefore measures have to change with them.

The fact that the likelihood of the plan being required is extremely small is the very reason why we have to be particularly prepared. If the personnel have not been trained and the disaster becomes reality, then a BCP is highly unlikely to work as intended. Regular tests are necessary to make personnel aware of how to act in the event of a disaster.

Secondly, every change that is made to the business processes must be included in the plan. An outdated plan will not help the organization to become operational again.

We can test as extensively as we like, from listening to the fire alarm to starting up a hot site or restoring a back-up. What is essential in all this testing, however, is that the procedures are tried out in a simulation of a real-life situation in order to see whether these measures are correct and effective.

> These sorts of matters also have to be arranged.
> Springbooks has arranged a redundancy site. So everything appears to be well organized. However, when fire broke out at the main office, it turned out that the redundancy site did not have any stores of official company letterheaded paper. The company had to wait for the delivery of the letterheaded paper before work could continue.
> Another example is that, while a stand-by arrangement is being used, a company still has to be accessible via its standard telephone number.

Personnel measures

A disaster may result in personnel problems if the people who support the primary process are also directly involved in the disaster and, as a consequence, are no longer available. Plans must include ways to replace these key people.

In the case of a major problem affecting the locality rather than just the company, staff may be unable to travel, particularly to a remote location

9.5 Springbooks

Springbooks is growing fast and recently their management decided to structure its approach to thinking about information security. For that reason an Information Security Officer has been appointed and has just started work with the company. His main task is to improve security within Springbooks and he has decided that his priority should be to implement an ISMS.

What are the first steps that the Information Security Officer should take?

In order to ensure that the personnel within Springbooks have a good understanding of information security the ISO commences a security awareness campaign. Given the geographical spread of organizational locations, what would be an effective way to organize this?

When looking at Springbooks, what would constitute a disaster for the business?

If this disaster occurs, what kind of plan would be needed to get the business up and running as soon as possible?

10. Managing communication and operating processes

10.1 Operating procedures and responsibilities

In order to maintain effective management and control of the IT of an organization, it is important to document procedures for the operation of the equipment and to assign responsibilities for required activities to the appropriate people. Details can be provided through work instructions, such as how computers are turned on and off, making back-ups, maintenance, processing mail, etc. A PC running on Windows can be forgiving if switched off incorrectly, whereas a Unix PC tends to respond quite differently. That's why procedures for starting up after a system failure are so important.

An operating procedure includes:
- How to deal with information;
- How, when and what back-ups are made;
- Contact persons in the event of an incident;
- Management of audit trails and log files.

The ultimate purpose of an operating procedure is to make sure there are no misunderstandings regarding the manner in which the equipment has to be operated. This is irrespective of whether it is a welding robot, a program that controls a power station or an accounting program.

The audit trail and system log files keep a record of all the events and actions on the system and network. These files are stored in a safe place and cannot, in theory, be modified. In the event of problems, these files are often crucial in discovering what went wrong. Consider the black box in an airplane which can establish what happened in the last few minutes before a crash. On the basis of this information, measures can be taken to ensure that the incident does not happen again.

10.2 Change management

The implementation of a change can lead to a catch 22 situation. Both implementing and not implementing the change involves a risk. This situation can arise, for example, in the case of a known vulnerability. Not installing a necessary patch is a risk as the vulnerability may be exploited and can lead to disruptions in the infrastructure. On the other hand, installing the patch is also a risk, as unforeseen circumstances (for example due to the stability of the systems) could lead to disruptions. This example also illustrates the necessity of defining different roles in the event of changes. For instance, the potential risk of not installing a security-related patch is determined by the Information Security Officer (ISO), whilst the risks associated with the change must be assessed by the manager of the system.

If changes have to be made to IT services and information systems, then these have to be carefully considered in advance and carried out in a controlled manner.

In IT Service Management, this process is called **change management.**

Change management manages changes in systems. These are often changes that have been planned in advance. An example of a small change is an alteration to a data table. A medium-sized change is, for example, the transition from Microsoft Office 'version 2' to Microsoft Office 'version 3'. A change has consequences that have to be understood and prepared for in advance. Personnel have to learn how to work with the new version. Standard forms have to be modified, and the service desk personnel have to be trained in order to be able to continue providing support.

A large change can be a change of production system, which would therefore require more preparation and organization.

Production systems should only be changed if there are substantive reasons to do so, such as an increased risk for the system. Updating systems with the latest version of an operating system or application is not always in the interest of a company, as this can sometimes result in greater vulnerability and instability.

This example shows why a segregation of duties is so important. If everyone were able to implement their own changes, an uncontrollable situation would arise in which people would not be aware of the changes implemented by others. Even more importantly, it would quickly become impossible to identify which change was responsible for any problems that might arise and, therefore, which change may need to be reversed.

10.3 Segregation of duties

Tasks and responsibilities must be segregated in order to avoid the chance of unauthorized or unintended changes, or the misuse of the organization's assets

In the segregation of duties, a review is conducted as to whether a person carries out decision-making, executive or control tasks. It is also determined whether the person needs access to information. Unnecessary access increases the risk of information being intentionally or unintentionally used, altered or destroyed. This is called the 'need to know' principle. The average employee at a company listed on the stock exchange, for example, does not have access to company information relating to its performance on the stock exchange, such as the expected profit and loss and annual figures. This prior knowledge could lead to insider trading, which is illegal.

Once personnel function and access needs are determined, tasks can be split up in order to reduce the risks for the organization. One example is the transfer of large amounts of money. One member of staff prepares the transaction and another authorizes the entry. There can be another member of staff who checks whether the transaction has been carried out correctly and legitimately.

It can be difficult for small companies to apply a segregation of duties, but this principle should be applied as far as is possible and practical. Page: 83

Where it is not practical to suitably segregate duties then alternative control measures should be investigated and implemented where possible.

10.4 Development, testing, acceptance and production

In order to ensure that changes cannot be implemented in an uncontrolled manner, it is also advisable to set up various (physical) environments for the development, testing, acceptance and production of information systems. There should be procedures to move software from one environment to the other. The option of keeping environments separate is not always possible for all organizations, indeed in smaller organizations it is possible the different environments are combined. For example this may involve combining development, testing and acceptance together, with production being kept separate.

For the development phase, specific security requirements apply. In the development environment the developers can create new software or work on changes to existing software. Versioning is very important.

The test environment is intended to determine whether the development meets the general requirements and, more specifically, the security requirements.

The acceptance environment is the environment in which end users can check whether the product meets their specifications. After acceptance, a system can then be put into production following set procedures. During the transition from the existing software to the new software, there must always be a fall-back plan so that, in the event of a major problem, it is possible to revert to the old version.

The production environment is intended to be used for production software and this is the environment in which end users normally work.

In the news

A customer of Springbooks discovered that anyone who knew his membership number and surname would be able to gain access to his personal data. Basically, it was possible to register on the Springbooks' website for a new online account, without it being checked whether the account already existed. Any person with malicious intent would then be able to enter in a new username, new password and new email address. A link would, in turn, be sent to this new email address enabling the fake customer to click on this and thereby activate a new account. The old account would still remain active, but, through these methods, others would be able to gain access to the customer's data. They would be able to see the person's address, telephone number and any requests made for deliveries, orders, Springbooks' Visa card, a new subscription, or a change of address notification.

A senior security consultant dealing in access and identity management said, "The error was an elementary one and would easily have been eradicated using Tmap® (a method for standardized testing). The fact that this was not done points to a sloppy process. The chances are therefore small that this is the only error. Writing software is still not yet a simple process, and writing a correct and secure software program is highly complex. What's more, in many projects insufficient attention is given to security. In some cases, people think that they can simply add it later. This fundamentally does not work. If you wish to secure data correctly then you have to give this the necessary attention, right from the moment that the functional specifications are established. Security must never be approached as if it were a project. It is a quality feature of a system. You must not only test whether an application does what it is supposed to do, but also whether it does not do what it should not do."

10.5 Management of services by a third party

Not all activities that are important to an organization are carried out by the organization itself. As soon as something is to be carried out by a third party, it is important to document the requirements that the party has to meet. For example, you would not ask a handy neighbor to fill in your tax returns, you would of course call upon the services of a tax consultant. You would assume that the tax consultant will handle your information confidentially; with a certified consultant this is required by a code of conduct.

When a company decides to outsource some or all of its IT, an effective contract has to be signed with the party providing this service in which all the security aspects are given the necessary attention.

In the news

One third of IT professionals misuse administrator passwords in order to find confidential information. A study conducted among 300 IT professionals has revealed that 33% secretly browse through the data of others, whilst 47% have on occasions looked at information that is not relevant to them.

"The only thing you need is the correct password or accounts with sufficient rights, then you can find out everything that is going on in a company." says Mark Fullbrook of Cyber-Ark. Administrator passwords are changed less often than user passwords. 30% are changed each quarter, whilst 9% are not changed at all. In this way, it is possible for employees who have left the organization to continue to have access to confidential information. What's more, half of the system managers do not require any authorization to gain access into accounts that have certain rights.

Springbooks' security policy has a special set of regulations for high privileged user accounts.

It is common practice to arrange a Service Level Agreement (SLA) in which both parties describe the services they expect to be carried out and under what circumstances. Audits are regularly carried out to see whether these agreements are being observed.

10.6 Protection against malware, phishing and spam

10.6.1 Malware

Malware is a combination of the words 'malicious' and 'software' and refers to undesired software such as viruses, worms, trojans and spyware. A standard measure against malware is to use anti-virus scanners and a firewall. It is, however, becoming increasingly clear that a virus scanner alone is not enough to stop malware. One of the main reasons for the outbreak of viruses is human actions. A virus infection can often occur by a user opening an attachment in an email that contains more than just the promised game, document or picture, but also a virus. It is therefore advisable not to open any suspicious emails or emails from unknown senders.

10.6.2 Phishing

Phishing is a form of Internet fraud. Typically the victim will receive an email asking him or her to check or confirm an account with a bank or service provider. Sometimes instant messaging is used and even telephone contact has been tried. It is difficult to catch up with the perpetrators of phishing. Internet users have to remain particularly vigilant and must never respond to an email request to transfer money or submit personal (financial) information, such as bank account numbers, PIN codes or credit card details.

In practice

Dear Springbooks Webmail subscriber,

We are currently undertaking maintenance on your springbooks.com account. This is our newest service to provide you with an even better service.

To complete this process you must give answer this message and give your current username here ( ) and password here ( ) if you are the correct owner of this account. Our Message Center will confirm your identity together with your secret question.

The new springbooks.com Webmail is a quick and simple application to enable you to access your emails. Also this process will help us to battle spam mails. Not giving your password, will make your email address inactive from our database.

You can also confirm your email address by logging on to your account at springbooks.com Webmail: https: / / webmail.springbooks.com

PLEASE NOTE: You s should end a password reset message in the coming seven (7) workdays after this process for security reasons.

thank you for using Springbooks.com Webmail!

https: / / webmail.springbooks.com

In the news

An attack on Springbooks' bookstore customers was discovered that attempted to steal not only bank details, but also credit card details, tax and social insurance numbers and PIN codes. This attack, which is possibly the work of a Dutch virus designer who struck previously via MSN, consisted of two parts, whereby malware changed the homepage of the victim. That page then linked to a hacked.nl domain. (According to the cache of Google, the domain tt-ribbons.nl).

The following text appeared on the hacked page page: "At present springbooks.com has been referred to the tax authority services in collaboration with google.nl and your ISP. It is compulsory for you to enter the requested details. The benefit for you is that for the next few years you will no longer have to send any tax returns as this will be done automatically by the new system of the tax authorities. It is important that you have the following products handy: identity card, cash card (of the account from which your orders are paid) and credit card."

The victims were even threatened: "Your IP address has been stored in the database springbooks.com," and the site showed the IP address of the visitor. In order to give this all a legitimate feel the site also featured a 'Hacker Proof' certificate and a Microsoft Certified Professional logo.

10.6.3 Spam

Spam is a collective name for unwanted messages. The term is normally used for undesired email, but undesired advertising messages on websites are also regarded as spam. The costs of spam are passed onto the recipients; compared to the very few people who are actually interested in these messages, the great majority waste a significant amount of time removing the messages from their mailbox.

A spam filter can ease the burden of this somewhat. There are also a few things that computer users can do to combat spam. Some of these are to never answer a spam message - even to 'opt out' or 'cancel' causes more spam as you are thereby confirming to the spammer that they have a working email for you and your spam will undoubtedly increase. Moreover, do not forward spam messages and do not distribute email addresses. To hide email addresses use the 'Blind Carbon Copy' (BCC) function, which is available in the email client.

In the news

By far, the great majority of messages sent in 2007 were spam. According to CleanPort, which measures the spam percentage in the Netherlands, 96% of the emails were undesired advertising.

When sending messages, the spammers often responded to current events. "In this way they hoped the recipients would be more inclined to open them," says CleanPort. In particular, political events that made big news caused an increase in the number of spam mails.

The measurements also revealed that much spam was sent as email attachments. This helped to by-pass spam filters. However, only 0.2% of these emails contained viruses. This could be because virus designers in 2007 concentrated more on delivering malware via web pages rather than of email.

Malware, phishing and spam are important subjects in the code of conduct and security awareness campaign for employees.

In the news

Many people these days order books via the Internet. It is convenient and safe. But there is also a downside. Criminals will always try to commit fraud through the Internet.

Internet shopping has experienced enormous growth in the last few years. Research carried out by the International Association of Webstores has shown that 98% of those who shop through the Internet regard it as safe. However, some 20% do not take enough security measures. Shops work on a daily basis to ensure they are secure, but the responsibility for security also lies with the consumer.

This led to the '3 rights' campaign in the Netherlands:

1. Is your PC security right?
2. Is the website of your bank right?
3. Is your payment right/correct?

Attentiveness can help to avoid a great deal of damage.

10.7 Some definitions

10.7.1 Virus

Definition:

A virus is a small computer program that purposefully replicates itself, sometimes in an altered form. The replicated versions of the original virus are, by virtue of this definition, also viruses. In order for the virus to spread it is dependent upon carriers that contain executable code.

Explanation:

As soon as the carrier is activated, the virus searches for new suitable carriers and tries to infect them. The virus can only spread outside the reach of the infected system if a user transfers files from the infected system to a new system.

Carriers were traditionally only programs, but these days documents can also act as a host for a virus as they increasingly contain executable codes, such as macros, VBScript, or ActiveX. In the great majority of cases, viruses are equipped with a payload that houses all tasks other than those that are necessary for replication. This payload is usually, but not necessarily always, destructive in nature.

Examples:

Brain
Chernobyl

Measures:

- Ensure that there is a virus scanner on the mail server and on the individual computers at the workplace. Always have a virus scanner with updated definitions;
- Ensure that the subject of viruses is included in a security awareness campaign;
- Ensure that this subject is included in the organization's information security policy;
- Ensure that there are effective ways of reporting incidents and that there are good follow-up procedures.

10.7.2 Worm

Definition:

A worm is a small computer program that purposefully replicates itself. The results of the replication are copies of the original spreading to other systems by making use of the network facilities of its host.

Explanation:

Although the differences between viruses and worms are becoming increasingly blurred, they still each have a number of distinctive features. A virus can attack its host via different carriers and infect new carriers by transferring active code in these new carriers. A worm in contrast does not depend on a user to spread itself; as soon as a worm is activated it can spread itself automatically. It is this that enables worms to infect large areas in a short period of time. The two most important similarities are the dependency on an executable code in the carrier and the use of a payload in order to carry out secondary, usually destructive, tasks.

Examples:

Melissa
I love you
Happy99
Blaster
Storm Worm

Measures:
- Ensure that there is a (virus) scanner on the mail server and on the individual computers at the workplace. Always have a virus scanner with updated definitions;
- As worms can be discovered in the network, ensure that you use a network monitoring tool;
- Ensure that the subject of worms is included in a security awareness campaign;
- Ensure that this subject is included in the organization's information security policy;
- Ensure that there are effective ways of reporting incidents and that there are good follow-up procedures.

10.7.3 Trojan

Definition:
A trojan is a program which, in addition to the function that it appears to perform, purposely conducts secondary activities, unnoticed by the computer user, which can harm the integrity of the infected system.

Explanation:
Just as with the real Trojan Horse, a trojan presents itself as something useful but, when activated by the user, it conducts all sorts of undesired activities in the background. The payload of a trojan often installs a 'backdoor', through which unknown persons can gain unauthorized access to the infected system. Another frequent activity of trojans is that they send confidential information from the infected system to another location where it can be collected and analyzed. The most noticeable difference with viruses and worms is that trojans cannot self-replicate. As a result, trojans are usually able to carry on doing their work unnoticed for a longer period of time.

Examples:
BackOrrifice
Netbus

Measures:
- Ensure that there is a trojan and/or virus scanner on the mail server and on the individual computers at the workplace. Ensure that the virus scanner is regularly updated;
- Ensure that the subject of trojans is included in a security awareness campaign; for example, staff must be aware of the dangers of opening attachments of suspicious emails;
- Ensure that this subject is included in the organization's information security policy;
- The consequences (communication-related) of trojans can also be discovered in the network by network managers; network monitoring tools are available for this;
- Another measure is the use of a personal firewall at the workplace itself in order to detect suspicious network traffic;
- Ensure that there are effective ways of reporting incidents and that there are good follow-up procedures.

10.7.4 Hoax

Definition:
A hoax is a message that tries to convince the reader of its veracity and then seeks to persuade the reader to carry out a particular action. The spread of a hoax depends on readers deliberately sending the message to other potential victims who may then also do the same.

Explanation:
The identification of a hoax is the first step in stopping the spread of a hoax. The payload of a hoax is not technical in nature but psychological. By playing upon peoples' emotions, the hoax tries to persuade the reader to send it to others (a form of social engineering). This is nearly always the purpose of a hoax, though it may on occasion try to convince a person to deposit money, provide personal information (phishing) or the like. Chain letters are the most significant and successful form of hoaxes. Chain letters (email) when sent to many others will consume mailserver resources, bandwith etc etc.

Examples:
Good times
Pen Pal

Measures:
- Ensure that there is a virus scanner at the workplace and an anti-spam solution for the mail server. A hoax often contains texts that can be recognized by such scanners;
- Ensure that the subject of hoaxes is included in a security awareness campaign; staff must be wary of strange questions in emails, particularly those that try to convince the reader to carry out certain actions like forwarding the hoax to others;
- Ensure that this subject is included in the organization's information security policy;
- Ensure that there are effective ways of reporting incidents and that there are good follow-up procedures.

10.7.5 Logic bomb

Definition:
A logic bomb is a piece of code that is built into a software system. This code will then carry out a function when specific conditions are met. This is not always used for malicious purposes. A computer programmer, for example, may build in a code which destroys (sensitive) files once they leave the company network. Viruses and worms often contain logic bombs, which usually have a built-in delay for the execution of the virus or the spread of the worm.

Measures:
For software written by company personnel or under contract with a third party, ensure that a code review is conducted by another party.

10.7.6 Spyware

Definition:

Spyware is a computer program that collects information on the computer user and sends this information to another party. The purpose of this is to make money. Spyware does not purposely try to damage the PC and/or the installed software, but rather to violate privacy.

Spyware can sometimes be recognized in a number of ways, for example:

- The computer is slower than usual;
- Programs are running on the computer that you have not started yourself or that you have never seen before;
- The settings on the computer have been modified and there may be a toolbar in your Internet browser that was not there before and cannot be removed;
- All sorts of pop-ups appear with no prompting or when opening web pages.

Measures:

- Ensure that the software at the work place is regularly updated;
- There are scanners that scan the windows registry for suspicious registry keys and scan the installed software for spyware. Sometimes anti-virus programs can detect spyware as well;
- Use a personal firewall in order to detect suspicious network traffic, especially traffic leaving your computer for no reason;
- Ensure that the subject of spyware is included in a security awareness campaign. Staff must be wary of strange questions in emails, particularly those that try to convince the reader to carry out certain actions;
- Ensure that this subject is included in the organization's information security policy;
- Ensure that there are effective ways of reporting incidents and that there are good follow-up procedures.

10.7.7 Botnets / Storm Worm

Since January 2007, the Internet has been plagued by the Storm Worm, a so-called botnet, which, according to various estimations, has infected millions of computers.

Storm Worm is patient, and therefore difficult to detect and analyze. It works like a colony of ants, whereby there is no central command and control server, but instead a network connection between thousands of infected PCs is set up. As a result, the infected machines do not affect the botnet. What's more, Storm Worm does not cause any damage or load to the host, so that the hosts do not know that they are infected.

The number of emails with links to virtual postcards or YouTube films that attempt to spread the Storm Worm is increasingly rapidly. On 15 August 2007 there was even an actual 'pandemic' when 600,000 emails were sent in less than 24 hours. This allowed the Storm Worm botnet to develop into a network that is estimated now to comprise millions of infected computers all over the world.

Although the text and title of the enticing messages for the Storm Worm are constantly changing, the email continues to contain a simple text or HTML code with a link to an IP address. That IP address provides a link to another infected machine within the botnet which immediately takes the user to a server in an attempt to infect the victim with Storm Worm.

The reason that Storm Worm has grown so rapidly is that the servers that spread the Storm Worm, recode the virus message every thirty minutes, changing the signature of the virus and making it difficult to detect by traditional anti-virus programs.

So why not simply disconnect the server, you may ask? Each computer on the Internet has an IP address and can be quickly traced. That is true, but these criminals are even quicker: just like with other botnets, the location of the computers that operate the botnet are protected behind a rapidly changing form of IP addressing (for the more technically-minded: the DNS technique 'fast flow'). The consequence is that the hosting site (where the Storm Worm is lying in wait) and the mail servers (which send the enticing messages) are difficult to detect and disconnect from the network.

As a result of the recent Storm Worm activities, the number of emails with a link to the infected code increased massively in August 2008 to 112.5%. This represented an increase of some 19% compared to the July figures, when 'contaminated' emails constituted only 0.5% of all emails.

Further analyses of web trends have shown that the number of suspicious websites is increasing hugely on a daily basis. In August 2007 an average of 1,772 new infected websites were detected and blocked every day. This represented a daily increase of 783 websites when compared to July 2007, only one month earlier.

Measures:
- Ensure that the software at the work place is regularly updated;
- There are scanners that scan the Windows registry for suspicious registry keys and scan the installed software for worms. Sometimes anti-virus programs can detect worm activity as well;
- Use a personal firewall in order to detect suspicious network traffic;
- Worms can also be discovered in the network; network monitor tools are available for this.
- Ensure that the subject is included in a security awareness campaign. Staff must be wary of strange questions in emails, particularly those that try to convince the reader to carry out certain actions. Suspicious websites should be avoided; there is a software indicating in your Internet browser when a website might be unsafe;
- Ensure that this subject is included in the organization's information security policy;
- Ensure that there are effective ways of reporting incidents and that there are good follow-up procedures.

10.7.8 Rootkit

A **rootkit** is a set of software tools that are often used by a third party (usually a hacker) after having gained access to a (computer) system. The rootkit hides itself deep in the operating system, possibly resulting in the operating system becoming unstable. A rootkit is almost impossible to remove without damaging the operating system.

Generally speaking, rootkits can work on two levels: the kernel level and the user level. Modern processors can handle programs in kernel mode and in user mode, and it is this difference that is fundamental: programs in kernel mode have access to the entire memory area whereas applications in user mode are limited to specific memory segments. Rootkits with kernel strategies can therefore do almost anything they want in the working memory. The purpose of these tools is to read, alter or influence the running processes, system data or files. A rootkit helps the intruder to gain access to the system, without the user noticing anything.

There are rootkits for almost every operating system. There are rootkits available for Linux, Solaris, Mac OS and most versions of Windows among others.

Rootkits became known more publically in the fall of 2005 when it came to light that the record company Sony/BMG incorporated rootkits in their music CDs in order to install an anti-copying security.

At the end of Augustus 2007, rootkits were introduced again to Sony products. This time it was in order to protect memory sticks. A rootkit was used in order to provide better protection, but unfortunately not enough attention was given to the further implications when applying this controversial security measure.

This security measure was actually not developed by Sony itself, but by the Taiwanese company FineArt Technology.

Rootkits are extremely difficult to detect, and can infect the system often without the user noticing anything. The sole purpose of a rootkit is to create and hide files, network connections, memory addresses and index entries. Even when the rootkit has been removed, the changes that the rootkit has made to the system remain unchanged and are usually undetectable. In other words, the only way to be totally sure that a rootkit has been removed is to format and reinstall the entire system from scratch. These days current anti-malware software is capable of detecting and removing active rootkits as well.

The name **rootkit** comes from the UNIX environment: **root** refers to the so-called super user in UNIX. In the 1980's, hackers succeeded in infiltrating UNIX systems and installing backdoors, which allowed them to repeatedly takeover the machine with root rights.

Measures:
- Ensure that the software at the work place is regularly updated;
- There are scanners that scan the Windows registry for suspicious registry keys and scan the installed software for rootkits. Sometimes anti-virus programs can detect rootkits as well, however it is recommended that you should use special tools that trace and destroy rootkits;
- Use a personal firewall in order to detect suspicious network traffic, rootkit software can make use of network traffic;
- Rootkits make use of the processor capacity and internal memory. Even though rootkits are well hidden, there are programs that can detect them;
- Ensure that the subject is included in a security awareness campaign. Staff must be wary of strange questions in emails;
- Ensure that this subject is included in the organization's information security policy;
- Ensure that there are effective ways of reporting incidents and that there are good follow-up procedures.

10.8 Back-up and restore

The purpose of making back-ups, or reserve copies, is to maintain the integrity and availability of information and computing facilities.

The consequences of the loss of information depend on the age of the information that can be retrieved from back-up. It is therefore important to consider the interval at which back-ups are made. How much time can we allow ourselves to generate again the information that has been lost. It is important that the back-up is tested regularly.

In addition to the actual creating and testing of back-ups, it is also necessary to consider how the back-ups are handled. Are the back-ups taken from a highly secure building and then placed in an unlocked cabinet? Or are the back-ups placed next to the server that contains the original data? Do the back-ups go to a third party? Is the data encrypted? For how long are the back-ups stored, and does this meet the statutory storage requirements?

10.9 Managing network security

A significant challenge in information security is that the shared network can extend beyond the boundaries of the organization.

In the news

The protection of private wireless networks in the Netherlands leaves a lot to be desired, as almost half of the networks investigated utilized WEP encryption that was easily decipherable or no encryption at all. During a war-drive carried out by Dimension Data, a total of 884 wireless networks were scanned, and the protection of private networks was examined. As many as 18% of the wireless networks were not protected at all and 28% used WEP (Wired Equivalent Privacy) that could be cracked within two minutes. The other 54% had WPA or WPA2 (WiFi-Protected Access) which is much more secure.

"Regardless of how safe you may feel your data is when you work at home on your PC, if you use a poorly protected wireless network, all the private data that you keep on your computer is at risk. Hackers can break into the wireless network and view all the information you keep on your laptop or PC. Private data such as bank account numbers, addresses and photos can therefore easily fall into the wrong hands," says a manager at Dimension Data.

Intranet - an intranet is a private network within an organization. For the user, the intranet is a private version of the Internet. The primary purpose of an intranet is the digital sharing of information within an organization. It can also be used for teleconferences and to facilitate and stimulate the digital collaboration within groups. Via a public network, such as the Internet, it is possible for an organization, to link together the separate parts of the intranet. Special encryption and decryption methods, along with other additional security measures, ensure the reliability of this transfer. When an organization makes part of its intranet accessible for customers, partners, suppliers or other parties outside the organization, this part is called an extranet.

Extranet - an extranet is a type of computer network within an organization. The extranet is related to the intranet. The purpose of extranet is to make company information securely available to customers, partners and suppliers outside the organization. For example, a company allows customers to place orders directly on the company network via the extranet. An extranet requires protection and privacy measures such as these to be used.
- A firewall;
- Digital certificates or other methods of user authentication;
- Encryption of the information in transit;
- VPNs (Virtual Private Networks) that communicate over the Internet.

VPN - a Virtual Private Network (VPN) makes use of an already existing network, usually the Internet, in order to enable information sharing between geographically separated networks as if it were on the company's own network. The data is effectively protected—thereby ensuring its integrity, authorization and authenticity—while it is being sent. Many technical protocols have been developed to ensure the availability of this service; currently, the most well-known and widely used protocol is IPsec.

In the news

An Australian security investigator has discovered a serious security leak in a coffee machine, whereby the attacker can change the taste and the amount of water for each cup. It is also possible to cause a Denial of Coffee, so that an engineer would have to be called out to repair the machine. The seriousness of the leak has been exacerbated by the fact that the coffee machine cannot be patched. The problem arose when the machine was fitted with an Internet Connection Kit.

Through this kit, which can be installed on Windows XP, the coffee machine can communicate with the Internet via the PC. This allows a user to download parameters in order to configure the espresso machine according to his or her own preference. In the event of a problem, an engineer can carry out remote diagnostic tests and provide a possible solution without the user having to leave the kitchen.

The investigator discovered that it is possible to remotely take over the XP system and software using the rights of the logged-in user. As far as we are aware, this vulnerability has not yet been exploited.

10.10 Handling media

Used here, 'media' refers to anything on which data can be recorded: paper, CDs, DVDs, USB sticks, hard disks, back-up tapes, BlackBerries, mobile phones, etc.

The purpose for having guidelines on how to handle media is to avoid valuable information getting into the wrong hands and to prevent the following consequences: unauthorized publication, change, deletion or destruction of assets or an interruption of business activities.

The manner in which the media must be handled is often linked to the classification or grading, and is documented in procedures. After the storage term has expired, files with sensitive information are put into the shredder or destroyed by a certified company. USB sticks are emptied, preferably using a 'wipe' tool that securely destroys the data. In addition, PCs ready for disposal are not simply thrown out with the garbage.

In practice

We always thought that a CD-Rom would last forever. In reality, however, after two to five years most of the CDs we have burned ourselves have lost so much quality that much of the data is unusable.

A number of important points:
- Media must be removed or deleted in a safe way if no longer required;
- System documentation and manuals must be kept in a secure place and updated regularly;
- The transport of media, which is of course packed well, should be carried out by a recognized courier firm that provides the correct physical conditions (humidity, temperature, electromagnetic protection).

> **In the news**
> Springbooks. has lost back-up tapes containing the data of at least 2.2 million customers.
> The data on the back-up tapes includes information about every customer over the last 16
> years. The tapes contain customer information, names, demographic information and many
> other sensitive items.
> A courier was supposed to transport the tapes, but an employee decided to take the tapes
> home in his own car. While in his house, they were stolen, probably by a burglar who
> thought it was a cashbox. The employee, who had worked for the company for 18 years, was
> dismissed.

10.11 Mobile equipment

Use of mobile equipment is growing exponentially and has ever-increasing capabilities. It is
therefore advisable to have rules in place for such equipment. Just think about the implications
of the loss of such devices. They are more than just hardware; they also contain software and
data. Many incidents occur that involve mobile equipment. Laptops are stolen from cars every
day. It is often simple to spot a laptop bag amongst other baggage at any airport, making things
easier for thieves. It is difficult to obtain insurance against this type of loss. Leave your mobile
equipment at work if possible, otherwise provide a suitable means of storage when travelling,
combined with insurance.

10.11.1 Procedures for handling information

Procedures must be developed for storing and handling information in order to protect it against
unauthorized publication or misuse. The best method for this is classification or grading. This
concept should be extended to mobile devices. Devices authorized to use more sensitive data
should be required to use stronger measure to protect against unauthorized access or the strongest
measures should be applied to all mobile devices.

Regulations must take account of the following areas:
- The position with regard to the general security policy of the organization;
- How, when and under what circumstances may classified information leave the organization;
- What classification or gradings are authorized for use;
- In addition to the grading, what designation can be used;
- How long is the grading valid for;
- Who is allowed to assign the grading;
- Under what circumstances and by whom can the grading be amended and/or terminated;
- Based on the grading, what are the confidentiality requirements;
- What security measures have to be applied in order to meet the confidentiality requirements.

> **In practice**
> A question that returns each year in Springbooks is how long it takes before the annual report
> will be made public? This documentcontains the annual accounts of the company. If the
> annual accounts were to be published too early, it could lead to insider trading in the stock
> market, which is illegal. That's why a company will take all the necessary steps to ensure that
> this information is kept secret right up to the moment of publication.

10.12 Exchanging information

In order to prevent information ending up with parties for whom it is not intended, it is important to develop and put in place internal and external agreements regarding information exchange. The purpose of the information exchange and to what the parties have actually agreed to should be documented. It can be stipulated how often information is to be shared and in what form.

It is important to prevent information from being exchanged between persons in different (possible competing) companies. Without clearly documented expectations, an employee or contractor may share sensitive information with the wrong party without realizing what detrimental effect this may have on the competitive position of their own company.

Increasing the awareness in this area is an important security measure.

> **In the news**
> An American Internet provider accidently deleted the email boxes of 14,000 customers. According to a spokesperson, this has never happened before and will never happen again. The spokesperson said that it was not possible to 'undelete' the lost data and offered her apologies.
> The mistake was a result of the provider, which also provides cable and telephone services, adhering to a practice of automatically removing inactive mail accounts every three months. In doing so on this occasion, it accidentally deleted these active accounts as well.

10.12.1 Electronic messaging

Electronic messaging has risks that are not present in the case of paper-based communication. That is why information exchanged digitally should be protected in an appropriate manner.

It is particularly important to be aware that when information is sent by email it can be read by anyone wishing to do so. What's more, copies of the email may be stored on servers spread all over the world. The Internet, after all, does not choose the shortest route, but the quickest route. The quickest route from London to Paris on a particular day may be via Moscow, New York and Berlin.

If information is highly confidential, it is best not to send it by email. If there is no other way, ensure first that you protect the message through encryption.

10.12.2 Systems for business information

When systems within a single company are connected to one another, procedures must be developed and implemented in advance in order to protect the information against unexpected security risks.

Although applications may be effectively protected individually, vulnerabilities can suddenly arise when they are linked. For example, in administration and book-keeping systems where information is shared between different parts of the organization. Vulnerabilities can also arise in the connections in company communication systems, such as telephone calls or telephone conferences, confidential telephone conversations, or the digital storage of faxes.

When (highly) confidential information is involved it is important to remember that most modern office printers—which are often combined with a scanner, fax and copy function—are equipped with a hard disk. This disk stores all the information that is to be processed. Through special applications, it is often possible to gain access to that hard disk and copy all the data on it. What's more, a 'maintenance engineer' could take that hard disk out of the building, often unnoticed.

In the news

An American security expert has discovered a method of sending print commands to network printers from websites. This technique could present unprecedented new possibilities for the spam industry.

Sending text to the network printer is child's play. A potential victim only has to open the site with fraudulent JavaScript. The problem is finding out the address of the network printer, but that can be solved by running through a few IP addresses using JavaScript. By looking at the IP address of the visitor, the number of IPs to be tried can be reduced to a relatively small number.

Once found, the printer is wide open to the whims of the spammer. Not only can simple texts be printed, but also fully laid out documents, all without the user noticing anything. "It is possible to change the print settings and even send faxes," says the expert.

A hacker even gives a few tips in a document on how to make malicious use of the leak: "Create a banner page. In this way every printout has your banner page added to it. This is a handy way to distribute your message."

This is possible in both Firefox and Internet Explorer. It does not work on printers that are directly connected to the computer and not on the network.

10.13 Services for e-commerce

When a company decides to set up an online shop, it will start to face completely new risks than when it used the Internet only to search for information. Services for e-commerce and its use must be effectively protected. Consider, for example, the requirement for secure payment transactions (Visa, MasterCard, IDeal, PayPal), the protection of information against fraud, clear conditions in contracts, non-repudiation of purchasing and indisputable prices.

The confidentiality and integrity of order transactions, payment information including credit card details, address details of the recipient and receipt confirmation must be guaranteed and the customers have to feel confident that no strangers can gain access to all this.

Information in online transactions must be protected in order to prevent incomplete transfers, incorrect routing, unauthorized changes, unauthorized publication, unauthorized duplication or display of messages.

In the news

When a customer of an Internet provider noticed that he had access to a very large file that he did not recognize, he downloaded it and found out that it contained all the customer details of an Internet provider, some two-and-a-half million in total. The manager probably made an error when creating the back-up file. The customer informed the service provider of this. When the Internet provider did not respond, he decided to share his experiences with an Internet forum.

"What happened here is wrong," said a spokeswoman from the Internet provider. "Normally this sort of notification would go to our security team, who would deal with it immediately."

Conclusions:

The first error was in the back-up procedure.

The second error was that the incident procedure was not followed, resulting in no response to this notification. It was only when the damage was done and the error became public that the provider responded.

Fortunately, in this case the person who made the discovery went no further than reporting this on a forum. He also could have published the entire list on the Internet, or could have sold the customer details, after which the customers concerned would have been inundated with spam or been placed at significant risk of identity fraud.

10.14 Publically available information

Company information that is presented to the entire world on an Internet page is public, but it still has to be correct and unable to be manipulated. Erroneous information will damage the reputation of the organization. It would be extremely annoying if you checked a company's website in order to find their bank details for a bill you had to pay, and then later discovered that it was incorrect and in order money had been deposited elsewhere.

It may be that information available on a public system—for example information on a web server that is accessible via the Internet—has to meet the legislative and regulatory requirements of the jurisdiction in which the system is located, the transaction occurred or the owner resides. It is also important that a computer program that has been made available meet the requirements of both the user and good security practice. Consider, for example, the computer programs provided by tax authorities for the submission of tax returns.

10.15 Summary

We now understand that policy provides direction on the way in which we set up information security. Policy is also used to demonstrate to government and other supervisory bodies that the legislative and regulatory requirements are being met. In addition, policy acts as an aid for employees whenever it is not clear what is or is not permitted.

We have also looked at the various organizational measures. How does the organization carry out the policy? What rules do personnel have to follow?

We now know what the PDCA cycle entails. The components of the ISO/IEC 27002 standard have been outlined and, in so doing, the relationship between the various aspects of information security has become clear.

We have explained what disasters are and how we can keep the risks that may result from disasters to a minimum by preparing for them.

Communication and operating processes, test procedures, in-house management or outsourcing of the IT environment have also been discussed.

We have also taken a closer look at malware and how we can protect ourselves against it.

The necessity of back-ups was examined. We looked at the security of the network and media and discussed the exchange of information and the subject of e-commerce.

10.16 Case study

Springbooks wishes to develop a greater presence in its home market. You have been hired as the Chief Information Security Officer (CISO) and have been given the task of ensuring that its customers are able to buy books through the Internet. The focus must be on the privacy of the customer. The customer must be able to conduct business, arrange and modify orders, create wishlists, view their bills, etc, on a twenty-four hours a day basis.

In order to show that it meets all the necessary security requirements, the company wishes to have itself certified.

You must ensure that the management knows everything that is going on and so can respond immediately to any problems. You are also responsible for ensuring that all personnel who are hired are reliable.

There must be alternative facilities available to take over immediately in the event of a disaster.

Provide a general outline of how you are going to develop an appropriate security infrastructure for Springbooks.

11 Law, regulations and standards

11.1 Introduction

Much has been said in the previous chapters about how and why information security is carried out. We have taken a close look at the risk analysis and determined a threat and risk profile. On the basis of this, we have undertaken physical, technical and organizational measures. Some measures are optional, whereas others are required by law.

Legislation covers the areas such as privacy, tax and finance and regulations for banks and companies with a listing on a stock exchange. A company's own policy must also be observed. With internationally operating organizations, it is possible that the policy has to be adapted in order to observe the legislation and regulations of other nations. Adhering to policy's and legislation is also known as compliance.

In chapter 9, the PDCA cycle was discussed. One of the components of that cycle is both self-monitoring (undertaken by internal audit) and monitoring carried out by an external auditor. These are components that involve ensuring adherence to internal and external legislation and regulations.

This chapter deals with the compliance to legislation and regulations and the manner in which the monitoring is carried out. The chapter will also provide an overview of some of the standards that are commonly used within the field of IT security.

11.2 Observance of statutory regulations

The primarily goal of every company is to achieve its own business objectives. This means producing a certain product or providing certain services. For example, the police and special investigation bodies ensure that certain legislation and regulations are observed. Every company, however, must observe local legislation, regulations and contractual obligations. The security requirements that a company must meet are closely related to these.

Although local legislation and regulations adhere to international agreements, it doesn't mean that they are designed to support internationally operating companies. These companies require a top level policy that is somewhat more general and whose underlying policy documents have to be adapted to the legislation in force in the country in which they are based, in order to do business locally. Legislative requirements may differ quite a bit, particularly in the area of privacy, and therefore the manner in which one deals with information that may be privacy-related should also differ.

In order to ensure that legislative and regulatory requirements are observed, it is always important to seek legal advice from the organization's local legal advisers or from qualified attorneys.

There is no one-size-fits all when it comes to regulations. There are for instance regulations that apply only to financial institutions and there are security regulations for the government. Governement specific regulations are usually country-specific and can include security regulations for special (sensitive or classified) information. Special information is a term for information that needs extra protection based on the sensitive nature that stems from its potential impact or risk to national security. For example the Europeans Commission classifies special information at five different levels. These levels are EU Top Secret, EU Secret, EU Confidential, EU Restricted, and EU Council / Commission. NATO also has five levels but uses slightly different terms. The five levels are Cosmic Top Secret, Focal Top Secret, NATO Secret, NATO Confidential and NATO Restricted.

11.3 Compliance

Compliance can also be described as tractability, obligingness, pliability, tolerance and dutifulness. What it boils down to is that an organization must observe its own internal regulations as well as the laws of the country and the requirements of local legislation and regulations.

Sometimes this can cause conflicts. A multinational organization, for example, has to adhere, on the one hand, to its internal policy, to ensure that the company operates consistently and is seen to do so and, on the other hand, to international and local legislation and regulations.

11.3.1 Personal data protection legislation

The right to privacy is a highly developed area of law in Europe. All the member states of the European Union (EU) are also signatories of the European Convention on Human Rights (ECHR). Article 8 of the ECHR provides a right to respect for one's "private and family life, his home and his correspondence," subject to certain restrictions. The European Court of Human Rights has given this article a very broad interpretation in its jurisprudence. In 1981 the Convention for the Protection of Individuals with regard to Automatic Processing of Personal Data was negotiated within the Council of Europe. This convention obliges the signatories to enact legislation concerning the automatic processing of personal data, which many duly did.

In order to understand the Directive, it is necessary to understand how and why EU and US perspectives on data protection and privacy are different. The United States prefers what is called a 'sectoral' approach to data protection legislation, relying on a combination of legislation, regulation, and self-regulation, rather than overarching governmental regulations. Former U.S. President Bill Clinton and former Vice President Al Gore explicitly recommended in their "Framework for Global Electronic Commerce" that the private sector should lead, and companies should implement self-regulation in reaction to issues brought on by Internet technology. To date, the US has no single, overarching privacy law comparable to the EU Directive. Privacy legislation in the United States tends to be adopted on an "as needed" basis, with legislation arising when certain sectors and circumstances require (e.g., the Video Protection Act of 1988, the Cable Television Consumer Protection and Competition Act of 1992, and the Fair Credit Reporting Act). Therefore, while certain sectors may already satisfy the EU Directive, at least in part, most do not

> The bookstore handles a variety of information that should comply to privacy legislation. Examples of such information are customer related information and employee related information. When processing this data the bookstore must make sure that it complies with regulations. It is important to know what laws and regulations apply to the data being processed within the information systems. In order to do this it is not only important to look at the information itself but also at the information systems that are used to process the data and the infrastructure that is used to transport the data. For the bookstore these analyses resulted in the maintenance of regional databases where customer data is being processed. One for the US, and one for the countries in which the EU privacy direction is applicable. Since there can be slight variations in the local implementation of this directive for countries within the EU local lawyers are consulted in order to ensure compliance in this area.

Compliance not only involves observing the legislation and regulations prescribed by governments, but the translation into internal rules also play an important role. In recent years, a worldwide standard for information security has been developed in the form of the Code for Information Security that was mentioned earlier. Derived from the British Standard BS 7799, an ISO standard has been developed and is known as ISO 27002 part of the ISO 27000.series. Various standardization bodies in the European Union and internationally have adopted this ISO standard. Thus, a far-reaching standard in security measures has been created for both government and business.

11.3.2 Compliance measures

As a result of the above, it has become clear that producing an internal policy within an organization is the way to become compliant. The first step for an organization is to produce a policy in which it declares that it must comply with the national and local legislation and regulations. In addition Procedures, guidelines and tools must be developed that make clarify the regulations and help employees to apply them in practice. Risk analyses must be conducted to ensure that the relevant risks are identified, the right security levels are set and the appropriate measures for those security levels are determined and implemented. Compliance is related to the field of security but is a specialized field of expertise. In order to achieve compliance it is important to work closely with legal experts.

11.4 Intellectual property rights (IPR)

When a company uses software, the use of material which could be subject to intellectual property rights must be considered.

The following guidelines need to be considered in order to protect material that may be considered intellectual property (it is important toalso bear in mind that copyrighted materials need to be addressed in order to be compliant to copyright legislation):

- Publish a policy relating to compliance with intellectual property rights, or copyrighted material, in which the legal use of computer programs and information products are defined;
- Maintain an awareness of the policy for the protection of intellectual property rights; include in the IPR policy the disciplinary measures the organization will take against any employees who violate this policy;
- Intellectual property rights include copyright to computer programs, documents, design rights, trade marks, patents and source code licenses;
- Only purchase computer programs from well-known and recognized suppliers to ensure no copyright is infringed;
- If open source is used, the associated license form must be respected and observed;
- Maintain a register of assets and identify the requirements of all of these assets in relation to the protection of intellectual property rights;
- Computer programs that are subject to intellectual property rights are usually supplied on the basis of a license agreement which states the license conditions.

One important aspect of IPR is to ensure adherence to license agreements. The bookstore Promotion Department periodically produces posters for store promotions, using photo processing software. Since there are five employees producing these posters, a package with five licenses of a particular computer software has been purchased. Each of the licenses is installed on a new PC and provided to the group of employees. The five new PCs also had photo processing software and there are five licenses. Then two new employees join the department, and both get their own PC onto which the photo processing software is installed as well. Due to the stress related to a project deadline, no-one found the time to purchase additional licenses. At that point there were seven PCs that have the same photo processing software, while licenses were purchased for only five PCs. This is an infringement of the license agreement and could result in fines.

Another form of intellectual property right infringement occurred when the department produced a poster with an image of Disney's Scrooge McDuk's safe. The use of an image is subject to copyright unless explicitly stated otherwise.

11.5 Protecting business documents

Important business documents need to be protected against loss, destruction and forgery, in accordance with statutory and regulatory requirements. The same applies, of course, to contractual obligations and business requirements. Registrations must be categorized according to type; for example registrations into the bookkeeping system, database records, transaction log files, audit log files and operational procedures.

For every type, the storage term and the type of storage medium has to be determined. For example, paper, microfiche, magnetic or optical storage may each be appropriate for different needs. Any cryptographic keys or computer programs that are associated with the encrypted archives or digital signatures also have to be stored in order to allow registrations to be deciphered throughout the required document retention period.

It is possible for the quality of the storage media to deteriorate over time. Therefore, procedures for the storage and handling of the selected media must be implemented in accordance with the manufacturers' recommendations. For long-term storage, the use of paper and microfiche should be considered.

Where electronic storage media are chosen, procedures need to be established to avoid information becoming lost as a result of future technological changes; it is important to guarantee that the information remains accessible (both the media and the data format must remain readable) during the entire storage period. Governments are subject to public records legislation. This legislation deals with the creation of archives, management, destruction, transfer to the central archive, transfer between governments and access to archives.

Recently the bookstore finally completed the upgrade of all their computer hardware systems. The fact that the latest laptops and PCs no longer have a diskette drive that reads 3 ½" diskettes became painfully clear, when for a financial statement needed to be produced and the required data was stored on these diskettes. It took quite some time to obtain the correct drive and read the data into the system. The bookstore learnt its lesson, namely that for data that really must not be lost, a more future-proof back-up and storage solution had to be introduced....

11.6 Protecting data and the confidentiality of personal data

The protection of data and privacy falls under personal data protection legislation and guidelines. In addition, contractual stipulations with a customer may also play a part. Every organization should have a policy for the protection of personal data and this policy should be known to everybody who processes personal data.

Observing this policy and all the relevant legislation and regulations for data protection can often best be achieved by appointing a person who is specifically responsible for the protection of data and who gives support to managers, users and service providers in the execution of their duties in this area.

Of course, there also has to be technical and organizational measures in place to protect personal data. It is important that the citizen has the right to inspect his or her registered data. Organizations should have a policy and procedures in place to ensure that this is the case.

11.7 Preventing abuse of IT facilities

One of the aspects that management must include in an information security policy is the manner in which the IT facilities should be used within the organization. Use of these facilities for non-business purposes—or any unauthorized purpose—without the permission of management should be regarded as improper use of the facilities.

If any unauthorized activity is observed through monitoring or otherwise, this activity needs to be brought to the attention of the manager in question in order to consider whether disciplinary and/or legal measures are to be taken.

There are, of course, two sides to such matters. On the one hand, the organization needs to fully meet the regulations mentioned above with regard to the correct use of licenses; namely to only use legal software and observe the rules surrounding intellectual property. On the other hand, staff are expected not to abuse the IT facilities made available to them.

In many organizations, there is now a code of conduct stipulating the rights and duties of the employer and of the employees in this area. It is, for example, often permissable to use the telephone and Internet for private means as long as the work does not suffer as a consequence. Downloading music, films and software and visiting sexually oriented sites are usually explicitly prohibited. The use of email should also be subject to conditions.

The employer has the right to monitor the use to which their systems are put. This may be done in the form of random checks or in a highly targeted manner when there is a strong suspicion of misuse by certain employees. This might be on the condition, however, that the employees are aware of the fact that these monitoring measures may be carried out. Conditions regarding such monitoring depend on the local legislation.

Prior to implementing such monitoring systems, it is important to gain legal advice and to consult the organization's council.

There is also legislation aimed at crimes conducted using computers. Intentionally gaining unauthorized access into a computer system is punishable by law, even if the system does not have any security. In recent years, computer criminality legislation has been tightened to counter attempts at making computer systems unusable through, for example, denial-of-service attacks. A denial-of-service is a method whereby an information system, for example a website, is inundated with requests until it can no longer cope with them and eventually fails. Botnets, networks of computers linked to one another, are often used for this sort of attack.

11.7.1 Computer criminality legislation

With the introduction of IT systems, specific IT crime or cyber crime also arose. In order to be able to prosecute cyber criminals it is important to have legislation that can be used. One of the problems with cyber crime law is that it is very difficult to develop world wide accepted laws, since cyber crime is not bound by the physical boundaries of a country or state. There are different laws worldwide there are different laws focusing on different aspects of cyber crime. There are laws addressing abuse such as spam and cyberstalking while others focus on computer fraud. All of this means that in cases where criminals are organized in a virtual worldwide organization, it takes a lot of effort and patience to be able to prosecute the bad guys. This doesn't mean that cyber crime is not prosecuted successfully, indeed there are numerous success stories in which cyber criminals have been put behind bars.

11.8 Observing security policy and security standards

Information security involves responsibility at different levels. The management board will always assume the final responsibility. It can, however, assign the responsibility for the execution and observance of the policy to the line managers. Managers, therefore, regularly need to assess (or have assessed) whether the data processing within their area of responsibility meets the applicable security policy, security standards and other security requirements.

> The bookstore has implemented the ISO/IEC 27002 standard. One of the security measures is applying password protected access to systems. The requirements for a password are stipulated in a password policy. The policy stipulates that, in order to gain access to the office computer system, a password of 8 characters has to be used. The password must not be a known word. What's more, it should contain at least 1 capital letter and 1 number or punctuation character.
> In an audit the auditor evaluates the set-up of the password measure and concludes that it is included in the policy. Next the the auditor tests whether it has been implemented: His conclusion is that the system manager has had the measure implemented into the system according to the required rules.
>
> The auditor looks at how it works in practice. He personally enters various passwords that do not meet the requirements. If the password is accepted then this security measure does not work correctly. If a password can only be entered if it meets the policy's requirements, then the measure works correctly.

11.9 Monitoring measures

Finally, the internal and/or external auditor will check whether the organization complies with the regulations. The auditor does this by looking at whether such a measure is in place. Is it included in the policy? Is it observed in practice? Does the measure function as it should?

11.10 Information system audits

Audits are useful as a means of periodically evaluating security measures, processes and procedures. Depending on the scope of an audit it can be used for different purposes. Audits can be applied to test whether security measures conform to defined requirements such as company standards, legislation and regulations. They are applied to evaluate if the security measures are in line with the security requirements specified for an information system. That these measures are implemented and maintained effectively. Finally audits help to verify that these measures are working as specified and expected.

In order to make sure that the importance of audits is sufficiently addressed, they should be part of an audit programme. Elements of an audit programme include, amongst others, the scope of the audits, audit criteria, frequency and audit methodologies. The plan should state what areas need to be audited, together with the outcomes of previous audits.

It is important to pay special attention to the selection of the auditors since they need to be objective in order to ensure impartiality of the audit process. One golden rule is that an auditor should never audit his own work. A documented procedure is needed that describes the responsibilities within a scope for defining the planning of and conducting of audits. The responsible manager should ensure that any non-conformities that are discovered are adequately addressed and that their causes are investigated. Furthermore he should ensure that required actions are taken and verify the results of these actions.

11.11 Protecting tools used for auditing information systems

The tools used for system audits, for example computer programs or databases, must be kept separate from development systems and production systems and should not be stored in tape libraries or users' rooms, unless additional protective measures of a suitable level have been taken. If third parties are involved in an audit, there is the risk that the audit tools and the information to which this third party has access may be misused. Measures to consider to help mitigate this risk include limiting access to only those systems that the auditor needs for his investigation, a Non-Disclosure Agreement and limiting physical access. Once an audit is complete, the organization should immediately change any passwords that were given to the auditors. Finally, after everything that has been discussed, one unchangeable rule will always apply: no matter how well an organization has planned its security, it is only as strong as the weakest link!

11.12 Standards and standards organizations

There are many organizations and standards about information security. Important standards are made by ISO, NIST and ANSI. In Europe ISO is most commonly used, whilst in the USA are the NIST and ANSI standards are more common. Most of the standards cover the same security objectives. However, each individual standard pays extra attention to a particular element within the discipline which they use to differentiate themselves from the other standards.

11.12.1 ISO

ISO, founded in 1947, is a worldwide federation of national standards bodies from some 100 countries, with one standards body representing each member country. The American National Standards Institute (ANSI), for example, represents the United States. Member organizations collaborate in the development and promotion of international standards. Among the standards the ISO fosters is Open Systems Interconnection (OSI), a universal reference model for communication protocols.

11.12.2 NIST

NIST (National Institute of Standards and Technology) is a unit of the US Commerce Department. The NIST 800 Series is a set of documents that describe United States federal government computer security policies, procedures and guidelines. The documents are available free of charge, and can be useful to businesses and educational institutions, as well as to government agencies.

NIST 800 Series publications evolved as a result of exhaustive research into workable and cost-effective methods for optimizing the security of information technology (IT) systems and networks in a proactive manner. The publications cover all NIST-recommended procedures and criteria for assessing and documenting threats and vulnerabilities and for implementing security measures to minimize the risk of adverse events. The publications can be useful as guidelines for enforcement of security rules and as legal references in case of litigation involving security issues.

11.12.3 ANSI

ANSI (American National Standards Institute) is the primary organization for fostering the development of technology standards in the United States. ANSI works with industry groups and is the U.S. member of the International Organization for Standardization (ISO) and the International Electrotechnical Commission (IEC).

Long-established computer standards from ANSI include the American Standard Code for Information Interchange (ASCII) and the Small Computer System Interface (SCSI).

Other important standards are developed by ITU and IEEE.

11.12.4 ITU-T

The ITU-T standing (for Telecommunication Standardization Sector of the International Telecommunications Union) is the primary international body for fostering cooperative standards for telecommunications equipment and systems. It was formerly known as the CCITT. It is located in Geneva, Switzerland.

11.12.5 IEEE

The IEEE (Institute of Electrical and Electronics Engineers) describes itself as "the world's largest technical professional society – promoting the development and application of electrotechnology and allied sciences for the benefit of humanity, the advancement of the profession, and the well-being of our members."

The IEEE fosters the development of standards that often become national and international standards. The organization publishes a number of journals, has many local chapters, and several large societies in special areas, such as the IEEE Computer Society.

Worldwide used protocols for connecting wireless networking are based on IEEE technology, like the A, B,G and N standards and the encryption standards WEP and WPA.

11.12.6 OWASP

Our coverage of standards ends with a very interesting initiative: the Open Web Application Security Project (OWASP). This is an open source application security project. The OWASP community includes corporations, educational organizations, and individuals from around the world. This community works to create freely-available articles, methodologies, documentation, tools, and technologies. The OWASP Foundation is a charitable organization that supports and manages OWASP projects and infrastructure.

OWASP is not affiliated with any technology company, although it supports the informed use of security technology. OWASP has avoided affiliation as it believes freedom from organizational pressures may make it easier for it to provide unbiased, practical, cost-effective information about application security. OWASP advocates approaching application security by considering the people, process, and technology dimensions.

OWASP is also an emerging standards body, with the publication of its first standard in December 2008, the OWASP Application Security Verification Standard (ASVS). The primary aim of the OWASP ASVS Project is to normalize the range of coverage and level of rigor available in the market when it comes to performing application-level security verification. The goal is to create a set of commercially-workable open standards that are tailored to specific web-based technologies. A Web Application Edition has been published, whilst a Web Service Edition is currently under development.

Even more interesting is the fact commerce using the Internet relies solely on trust; users will not use systems that they believe are insecure. The Payment Card Industry (PCI) compliance is mandatory for merchants, third party processors, and service bureaus - not optional. PCI has adopted OWASP as the de facto standard for securing payment cards.

11.13 Summary

In this chapter we have discussed the role of legislation and regulations. There is legislation for tax matters, for privacy and for how business is conducted. There is local legislation, international legislation and regulations such as the Sarbanes-Oxley Act which stipulates that each foreign corporation that is listed on the New York Stock Exchange must demonstrate that it conforms with American legislation and regulations.

We have seen that standards such as the ISO/IEC 27002 help in observing the legislation and regulations.

Intellectual property rights of others must be protected in just the same way as the property of the organization. If a company has invested hundreds of thousands, maybe even millions in the development of a product, it naturally does not want anyone to copy it without permission and to offer it at a lower price.

Finally, an audit can demonstrate that the requirements for the security of the information are being successfully met.

11.14 Case study

Incasso Services is a large debt-collection agency that is responsible for the collection of late payments for a large number of customers including Springbooks. Incasso Services started as a sole trader and has developed over the years into a company with five offices in the Benelux countries (Belgium, the Netherlands and Luxembourg) that also offers banking services, albeit on a small scale. The company has 60 employees.

In order to address extensive legislation and regulations, you have been hired to ensure that information security is implemented in accordance with the ISO/IEC 27002 standard. You will investigate what legislation and regulations apply and, based on this information, will produce the policy.

To prove the efficacy of your program, you must commission an external audit to demonstrate that your program being properly followed.

Describe what you have to do to develop the security plan. Outline which security measures have to be carried out. How will you show the auditors that your company has arranged everything properly? What legislation and regulations prescribed by the government must you deal with? Describe what standards you could use and how you would apply them in this case?

Appendix A Glossary

The glossary contains an explanation of concepts in relation to information security which appear in the text, where they are discussed in greater detail. The list is not exhaustive. It can be used as a tool in order to enhance the readers' understanding of the terminology applied in this book.

Availability:	ensures the reliable and timely access to data or computing resources by the appropriate personnel. In other words, availability guarantees that the systems are up and running when needed. In addition, this concept guarantees that the security services required by the security practitioner are in working order.
Due care:	shows that a company has taken responsibility for the activities that take place within the corporation and has taken the necessary steps to help protect the company, its resources, and employees from possible threats.
Due diligence:	the act of investigating and understanding the risks the company (or governmental organization) faces. A company practices due care by developing and implementing security policies, procedures, and standards.
Evaluation:	process of comparing the estimated risk against given risk criteria to determine the significance of the risk.
Exposure:	an exposure is an instance of being exposed to losses from a threat agent. A vulnerability exposes an organization to possible damages.
Hoax:	a hoax is a message that tries to convince the reader of its veracity and then persuades the reader to carry out a particular action. The spread of a hoax depends on readers deliberately sending the message to other potential victims who may then also do the same.
Information architecture:	the definition of an architecture as used in ANSI/IEEE Standard 1471-2000 is: "The fundamental organization of a system, embodied in its components, their relationships to each other and the environment, and the principles governing its design and evolution."
Logic bomb:	a piece of code that is built into a software system. This code will then carry out a function when specific conditions are met. This is not always used for malicious purposes. A computer programmer, for example, may build in a code which destroys (sensitive) files once they leave the company network. Viruses and worms often contain logic bombs, which usually have a built-in delay for the execution of the virus or the spread of the worm.
Risk:	the likelihood of a threat agent taking advantage of a vulnerability and the corresponding business impact.
Risk analysis:	systematic use of information to identify sources and to estimate the risk.
Risk assessment:	overall process of risk analysis and risk evaluation.

Risk avoidance: the measures taken are so that the threat is neutralized to such an extent that the threat no longer leads to an incident. Consider, for example, the software patches for an operating system. By patching the OS immediately after the patches are available, you are preventing your system against know technical problems or security issues. Many of the countermeasures within this strategy have a preventive character.

Risk bearing: recognition of the fact that certain risks are accepted. This could be because the costs of the security measures exceed the possible damage. But it could also be that the management decides to do nothing even if the costs are not higher than the possible damage. The measures that a risk bearing organization takes in the area of information security are usually of a repressive nature.

Risk management: the process of planning, organizing, leading, and controlling the activities of an organization in order to minimize the effects of risk on an organization's capital and earnings.

Risk neutral: the security measures taken are such that the threats either no longer manifest themselves or, if they do, the resulting damage is minimized. The majority of measures taken in the area of information security by a risk neutral organization are a combination of preventive, detective and repressive measures.

Risk treatment: the process of selection and implementation of measures to modify risk.

Rootkit: a set of software tools that are often used by a third party (usually a hacker) after having gained access to a (computer) system. The rootkit hides itself deep in the operating system, possibly resulting in the operating system becoming unstable. A rootkit is almost impossible to remove without damaging the operating system.

Security control: security controls are measures taken to safeguard an information system from attacks against the confidentiality, integrity, and availability (CIA) of the information system. Note that the terms safeguard and countermeasure are sometimes used as synonyms for security control.

Spyware: a computer program that collects information on the computer user and sends this information to another party. The purpose of this is to make money. Spyware does not purposely try to damage the PC and/or the installed software, but rather to violate privacy.

Storm Worm: since January 2007, the Internet has been plagued by the Storm Worm, a so-called botnet, which, according to various estimations, has infected millions of computers.

Threat: a potential cause of an unwanted incident, which may result in harm to a system or organization.

Threat agent: the entity that takes advantage of a vulnerability is referred to as a threat agent.

Trojan:	a trojan is a program which, in addition to the function that it appears to perform, purposely conducts secondary activities, unnoticed by the computer user, which can harm the integrity of the infected system.
Virus:	a small computer program that purposefully replicates itself, sometimes in an altered form. The replicated versions of the original virus are, by virtue of this definition, also viruses. In order for the virus to spread it is dependent upon carriers that contain executable code.
Vulnerability:	a weakness of an asset or group of assets that can be exploited by one or more threats.
Worm:	a small computer program that purposefully replicates itself. The results of the replication are copies of the original spreading to other systems by making use of the network facilities of its host.

Appendix B1 Sample exam Information Security Foundation based on ISO/IEC 27002

Introduction

This is a sample exam from the Information Security Foundation based on ISO/IEC 27002.

This sample exam consists of 40 multiple-choice questions. Each multiple-choice question has a number of possible answers, of which only one is the correct answer.

The maximum number of points that can be obtained for this exam is 40. Each correct answer is worth one point. If you obtain 26 points or more you will pass.

The time allowed for this exam is 60 minutes.

No rights may be derived from this information.

Good luck!

Sample exam

1 of 40

You have received a draft of your tax return from the accountant and you check whether the data is correct.

Which characteristic of reliability of information are you checking?
A. availability
B. exclusivity
C. integrity
D. confidentiality

2 of 40

In order to take out a fire insurance policy, an administration office must determine the value of the data that it manages.

Which factor is **not** important for determining the value of data for an organization?
A. The content of data.
B. The degree to which missing, incomplete or incorrect data can be recovered.
C. The indispensability of data for the business processes.
D. The importance of the business processes that make use of the data.

3 of 40

Our access to information is becoming increasingly easy. Still, information has to be reliable in order to be usable.

What is **not** a reliability aspect of information?
A. availability
B. integrity
C. quantity
D. confidentiality

4 of 40

"Completeness" is part of which aspect of reliability of information?
A. availability
B. exclusivity
C. integrity
D. confidentiality

5 of 40

An administration office is going to determine the dangers to which it is exposed.

What do we call a possible event that can have a disruptive effect on the reliability of information?
A. dependency
B. threat
C. vulnerability
D. risk

6 of 40

What is the purpose of risk management?
A. To determine the probability that a certain risk will occur.
B. To determine the damage caused by possible security incidents.
C. To outline the threats to which IT resources are exposed.
D. To use measures to reduce risks to an acceptable level.

7 of 40

Which statement about risk analysis is correct?
1. Risks that are stated in a risk analysis can be classified.
2. In a risk analysis all details have to be considered.
3. A risk analysis limits itself to availability.
4. A risk analysis is simple to carry out by completing a short standard questionnaire with standard questions.

A. 1
B. 2
C. 3
D. 4

8 of 40

Which of the examples given below can be classified as fraud?
1. Infecting a computer with a virus.
2. Carrying out an unauthorized transaction.
3. Tapping communication lines and networks.
4. Using the work internet for private ends.

A. 1
B. 2
C. 3
D. 4

9 of 40

A possible risk for a company is fire damage. If this threat occurs, that is to say that a fire actually breaks out, direct and indirect damage may result.

What is an example of direct damage?
A. a database is destroyed
B. image loss
C. loss of client trust
D. statutory obligations can no longer be met

10 of 40

In order to reduce risks, a company decides to opt for a strategy of a mix of measures. One of the measures is extinguishing a fire.

To which category of measures does extinguishing a fire belong?
A. corrective measures
B. detective measures
C. preventive measures
D. repressive measures

11 of 40

What is an example of a human threat?
A. A USB-stick passes on a virus to the network.
B. Too much dust in the server room.
C. A leak causes a failure of electricity supply.

12 of 40

What is an example of a human threat?
A. a lightning strike
B. fire
C. phishing

13 of 40

Information has a number of reliability aspects.
Reliability is constantly being threatened. Examples of threats are: a cable becomes loose, someone alters information by accident, data is used privately or is falsified.

Which of these examples is a threat to confidentiality?
A. a loose cable
B. accidental deletion of data
C. private use of data
D. falsifying data

14 of 40

A member of staff denies sending a particular message.

Which reliability aspect of information is in danger here?
A. availability
B. correctness
C. integrity
D. confidentiality

15 of 40

In the incident cycle there are four successive steps.

What is the order of these steps?
A. Threat, Damage, Incident, Recovery
B. Threat, Incident, Damage, Recovery
C. Incident, Threat, Damage, Recovery
D. Incident, Recovery, Damage, Threat

16 of 40

A fire breaks out in a branch office of a health insurance company. The personnel are transferred to neighboring branches to continue their work.

Where in the incident lifecycle are such stand-by arrangements found?
A. between threat and incident
B. between recovery and threat
C. between damage and recovery
D. between incident and damage

17 of 40

How is the purpose of an information security policy best described?
A. Policy documents the analysis of risks and the search for countermeasures.
B. Policy provides direction and support to the management regarding information security.
C. Policy makes the security plan concrete by providing it with the necessary details.
D. Policy provides insight into threats and the possible consequences.

18 of 40

The code of conduct for e-business is based on a number of principles.

Which of the following principles do **not** belong?
A. reliability
B. registration
C. confidentiality and privacy

19 of 40

A worker from insurance company Euregio discovers that the expiration date of a policy has been changed without her knowledge. She is the only person authorized to do this. She reports this security incident to the Helpdesk. The Helpdesk worker records the following information regarding this incident:

• date and time
• description of the incident
• possible consequences of the incident

What important information about the incident is missing here?
A. the name of the person reporting the incident
B. the name of the software package
C. the PC number
D. a list of people who were informed about the incident

20 of 40

A company experiences the following incidents:
1. A smoke alarm does not work.
2. The network is hacked into.
3. Someone pretends to be a member of staff.
4. A file on the computer cannot be converted into a PDF file.

Which of these incidents is **not** a security incident?
A. 1
B. 2
C. 3
D. 4

21 of 40

Security measures can be grouped in various ways.

Which of the following is correct?
A. physical, logical, preventive
B. logical, repressive, preventive
C. organizational, preventive, corrective, physical
D. preventive, detective, repressive, corrective

22 of 40

A smoke alarm is placed in a computer room.

Under which category of security measures does this fall?
A. corrective
B. detective
C. organizational
D. preventive

23 of 40

The Information Security Officer (ISO) of insurance company Euregio wishes to have a list of security measures put together.

What does he first have to do before security measures can be selected?
A. Set up monitoring.
B. Carry out an evaluation.
C. Formulate information security policy.
D. Carry out a risk analysis.

24 of 40

What is the purpose of classifying information?
A. To determine what types of information may require different levels of protection.
B. To allocate information to an owner.
C. To reduce the risks of human error.
D. To prevent unauthorized access to information.

25 of 40

Strong authentication is needed to access highly protected areas. In case of strong authentication the identity of a person is verified by using three factors.

Which factor is verified when we must enter a personal identification number (PIN)?
A. something you are
B. something you have
C. something you know

26 of 40

Access to the computer room is closed off using a pass reader. Only the System Management department has a pass.

What type of security measure is this?
A. a corrective security measure
B. a physical security measure
C. a logical security measure
D. a repressive security measure

27 of 40

Four (4) staff members of the IT department share one (1) pass for the computer room.

What risk does this lead to?
A. If the power fails, the computers go off.
B. If fire breaks out the fire extinguishers can not be used.
C. If something disappears from the computer room it will not be clear who is responsible.
D. Unauthorized persons may gain access to the computer room without being seen.

28 of 40

In the reception hall of an administration office, there is a printer which all staff can use in case of emergency. The arrangement is that the printouts are to be collected immediately so that they cannot be taken away by a visitor.

What other risk for the company information does this situation have?
A. Files can remain in the memory of the printer.
B. Visitors would be able to copy and print out confidential information from the network.
C. The printer can become defective through excessive use, so that it is no longer available for use.

29 of 40

Which of the following security measures is a technical measure?

1. Allocating information to an owner
2. Encryption of files
3. Creating a policy defining what is and is not allowed in e-mail
4. Storing system management passwords in a safe

A. 1
B. 2
C. 3
D. 4

30 of 40

The back-ups of the central server are kept locked in the same enclosed room as the server.

What risk does the organization face?
A. If the server crashes, it will take a long time before the server is again operational.
B. In the event of fire it is impossible to get the system back to its former state.
C. No one is responsible for the back-ups.
D. Unauthorized persons have easy access to the back-ups.

31 of 40

Which of the following technologies is malicious?
A. encryption
B. hash
C. Virtual Private Network (VPN)
D. viruses, worms and spyware

32 of 40

Which measure does **not** help against malicious software?
A. an active patch policy
B. an anti-spyware program
C. a spam filter
D. a password

33 of 40

What is an example of an organizational measure?
A. back-up of data
B. encryption
C. segregation of duties
D. keeping network equipment and junction boxes in a locked room

34 of 40

Identification is establishing whether someone's identity is correct.

Is this statement correct?
A. yes
B. no

35 of 40

Why is it necessary to keep a disaster recovery plan up to date and to test it regularly?
A. In order always to have access to recent back-ups that are located outside the office.
B. In order to be able to cope with daily occurring faults.
C. Because otherwise, in the event of a far-reaching disruption, the measures taken and the incident procedures planned may not be adequate or may be outdated.
D. Because this is required by the Personal Data Protection Act.

36 of 40

What is authorization?
A. The determination of a person's identity.
B. The registration of actions carried out.
C. The verification of a person's identity.
D. The granting of specific rights, such as selective access to a person.

37 of 40

Which important statutory norm in the area of information security do government bodies have to comply with?
A. Dependency & Vulnerability analysis
B. ISO/IEC 20000
C. ISO/IEC 27002
D. national information security legislation or regulations

38 of 40

On the basis of which legislation can someone request to inspect the data that has been registered about him or her?
A. The Public Records Act
B. The Personal Data Protection Act
C. The Computer Criminality Act
D. The Government Information (Public Access) Act

39 of 40

The Code for Information Security (ISO/IEC 27002) is a description of a risk analysis method.

Is this statement correct?
A. yes
B. no

40 of 40

The Code for Information Security (ISO/IEC 27002) only applies to large companies.

Is this statement correct?
A. yes
B. no

Appendix B2 Evaluation

The table below shows the correct answers to the questions in the sample examination.

number	answer	points
1	C	1
2	A	1
3	C	1
4	C	1
5	B	1
6	D	1
7	A	1
8	B	1
9	A	1
10	A	1
11	A	1
12	C	1
13	C	1
14	C	1
15	B	1
16	D	1
17	B	1
18	B	1
19	A	1
20	D	1

number	answer	points
21	D	1
22	B	1
23	D	1
24	A	1
25	C	1
26	B	1
27	C	1
28	A	1
29	B	1
30	B	1
31	D	1
32	D	1
33	C	1
34	B	1
35	C	1
36	D	1
37	D	1
38	B	1
39	B	1
40	B	1

Appendix B3   Answer key to the sample exam

1 of 40

You have received a draft of your tax return from the accountant and you check whether the data is correct.
Which characteristic of reliability of information are you checking?
A. availability
B. exclusivity
C. integrity
D. confidentiality

A. Incorrect. Availability is the degree to which information is available for the users at the required times. This information is right now available, so it is not an issue.
B. Incorrect. Exclusivity is a characteristic of confidentiality. The confidentiality of the correspondence is guaranteed by the post.
C. **Correct.** This concerns integrity. See section 4.1.2 of "*Foundations of IT Security*". 'Integrity refers to being correct or consistent with the intended state of information. Any unauthorized modification of data, whether deliberate or accidental, is a breach of data integrity'
D. Incorrect. Answers B and D are statements of the same concept. This concerns the degree to which the access to information is restricted to only those who are authorized.

2 of 40

In order to take out a fire insurance policy, an administration office must determine the value of the data that it manages.
Which factor is not important for determining the value of data for an organization?
A. The content of data.
B. The degree to which missing, incomplete or incorrect data can be recovered.
C. The indispensability of data for the business processes.
D. The importance of the business processes that make use of the data.

A. **Correct.** The content of data does not determine its value. See section 4.5.4 of "*Foundations of IT Security*". Data can have great significance – depending on how it is used – even if it isn't in the format of 'information' as defined earlier. There would be no need for 'data protection' and hence 'computer security' if data by definition had no significance. The value of data is determined primarily by the user.
B. Incorrect. Missing, incomplete or incorrect data that can be easily recovered is less valuable than data that is difficult or impossible to recover.
C. Incorrect. Indispensable data is very important for business processes. It is part of determining the value of data and makes part of the decision what has to be insured.
D. Incorrect. Data critical to important business processes is therefore valuable.

3 of 40

Our access to information is becoming increasingly easy. Still, information has to be reliable in order to be usable.
What is **not** a reliability aspect of information?
A. availability
B. integrity
C. quantity
D. confidentiality

A. Incorrect. Availability is a reliability aspect of information. See section 4.1.3 of *"Foundations of IT Security"*. The information is available when needed.
B. Incorrect. Integrity is a reliability aspect of information.
C. **Correct.** Quantity is not a reliability aspect of information. See section 4 of *"Foundations of IT Security"*. Besides confidentiality, integrity and availability, are possession, control, authenticity and utility concepts being used in information security. (See section 4.3 of *"Foundations of IT Security"* Parkerian Hexad.) Quantity is not part of these concepts.
D. Incorrect. See section 4.1.1 of *"Foundations of IT Security"*. Confidentiality is a reliability aspect of information. Confidentiality, refers to limits on who can get what kind of information.

4 of 40

"Completeness" is part of which aspect of reliability of information?
A. availability
B. exclusivity
C. integrity
D. confidentiality

A. Incorrect. See section 4.1.3 of *"Foundations of IT Security"*. The information is available when needed; information may be available without having to be complete.
B. Incorrect. See section 4.1.1 of *"Foundations of IT Security"*. Confidentiality is a reliability aspect of information. Confidentiality, refers to limits on who can get what kind of information. Exclusivity is a characteristic of confidentiality.
C. **Correct.** See section 4.1.2 of *"Foundations of IT Security"*. 'Integrity refers to being correct or consistent with the intended state of information. Any unauthorized modification of data, whether deliberate or accidental, is a breach of data integrity'. Completeness is part of the integrity aspect.
D. Incorrect. See section 4.1.1 of *"Foundations of IT Security"*. Confidentiality is a reliability aspect of information. Confidentiality, refers to limits on who can get what kind of information. Confidential information does not have to be complete.

5 of 40

An administration office is going to determine the dangers to which it is exposed.
What do we call a possible event that can have a disruptive effect on the reliability of information?
A. dependency
B. threat
C. vulnerability
D. risk

A. Incorrect. A dependency is not an event. A data dependency in computer science is a situation in which a program statement (instruction) refers to the data of a preceding statement. This has nothing to do with information security.
B. **Correct**. See section 5.1.2 of "*Foundations of IT Security*". A threat is a potential cause of an unwanted incident, which may result in harm to a system or organization.
C. Incorrect. See section 5.1.1 of "*Foundations of IT Security*" A vulnerability is a weakness of an asset or group of assets that can be exploited by one or more threats.
D. Incorrect. See section 5.1.3 of "*Foundations of IT Security*". A risk is the likelihood of a threat agent taking advantage of a vulnerability and the corresponding business impact.

6 of 40

What is the purpose of risk management?
A. To determine the probability that a certain risk will occur.
B. To determine the damage caused by possible security incidents.
C. To outline the threats to which IT resources are exposed.
D. To use measures to reduce risks to an acceptable level.

A. Incorrect. See section 5.5 of "*Foundations of IT Security*". This is part of risk analysis. "Risk analysis is the process of defining and analyzing the dangers to individuals, businesses and government agencies posed by potential natural and human-caused adverse events.
B. Incorrect. See section 5.5 of "*Foundations of IT Security*". This is part of risk analysis. "Risk analysis is the process of defining and analyzing the dangers to individuals, businesses and government agencies posed by potential natural and human-caused adverse events.
C. Incorrect. See section 5.5 of "*Foundations of IT Security*". This is part of risk analysis. See section 5.1.2 Threat, of "Foundations of IT Security". A threat is a potential cause of an unwanted incident, which may result in harm to a system or organization. The entity that takes advantage of a vulnerability is referred to as a threat agent.
D. **Correct**. See section 5.4 of "*Foundations of IT Security*". Risk management is the process of planning, organizing, leading, and controlling the activities of an organization in order to minimize the effects of risk on an organization's capital and earnings.

7 of 40

Which statement about risk analysis is correct?
1. Risks that are stated in a risk analysis can be classified.
2. In a risk analysis all details have to be considered.
3. A risk analysis limits itself to availability.
4. A risk analysis is simple to carry out by completing a short standard questionnaire with standard questions.

A. 1
B. 2
C. 3
D. 4

A. **Correct.** Not all risks are equal. As a rule the largest risks are tackled first. See section 5.9 of "*Foundations of IT Security*" about types of risk strategies.
B. Incorrect. It is impossible in a risk analysis to examine every detail.
C. Incorrect. A risk analysis considers all reliability aspects, including integrity and confidentiality along with availability.
D. Incorrect. In a risk analysis questions are seldom applicable to every situation and need to be in accordance with the corporate culture.

8 of 40

Which of the examples given below can be classified as fraud?
1. Infecting a computer with a virus.
2. Carrying out an unauthorized transaction.
3. Tapping communication lines and networks.
4. Using the work internet for private ends.

A. 1
B. 2
C. 3
D. 4

A. Incorrect. See section 10.6 of "*Foundations of IT Security*". Malware is a combination of the word Malicious and Software and refers to undesired software such as viruses, worms, trojans and spyware. And see section 4.1.2 "*Foundations of IT Security*", a virus infection is classified as the threat "unauthorized change". When an attacker inserts a virus, logic bomb, or back door into a system, the system's integrity is compromised. This can, in turn, negatively affect the integrity of information held on the system by corruption, malicious modification, or replacement of data with incorrect data. Strict access controls, intrusion detection, and hashing can combat these threats.
B. **Correct.** See section 9.2.4 'In the news' of "*Foundations of IT Security*". An unauthorized transaction is classified as "fraud". In the broadest sense, a fraud is an intentional deception made for personal gain or to damage another individual.

C. Incorrect. See section 4.1.1 of "*Foundations of IT Security*". Confidentiality ensures that the *necessary level of secrecy is enforced at each element of data processing* and prevents unauthorized disclosure. Tapping is classified as the threat "disclosure".

D. Incorrect. See section 9.2 of "*Foundations of IT Security*". Private use is classified as the threat "misuse".

9 of 40

A possible risk for a company is fire damage. If this threat occurs, that is to say that a fire actually breaks out, direct and indirect damage may result.
What is an example of direct damage?

A. a database is destroyed
B. image loss
C. loss of client trust
D. statutory obligations can no longer be met

A. **Correct**. A destroyed database is an example of direct damage. See section 5.8 of "*Foundations of IT Security*".
   Damage as a result of the manifestation of the above threats can be classified into two groups:
   1. Direct damage
   2. Indirect damage
   An example of direct damage is theft. Theft has direct consequences on the business.
   Indirect damage is consequential loss that can occur.
   Another example is damage caused by the water from fire extinguishers or being unable to meet a contract due to the IT infrastructure being destroyed by fire.

B. Incorrect. See section 5.8 of "*Foundations of IT Security*". Indirect damage is consequential loss that can occur. An example of indirect damage is being unable to meet a contract due to the IT infrastructure being destroyed by fire, or loss of goodwill by unintentional failure to fulfill contractual obligations.

C. Incorrect. Loss of client trust is indirect damage which follows after a disaster occurred, just like the answer B.

D. Incorrect. Being unable to meet statutory obligations is indirect damage.

10 of 40

In order to reduce risks, a company decides to opt for a strategy of a mix of measures. One of the measures is extinguishing a fire.
To which category of measures does extinguishing a fire belong?
A. corrective measures
B. detective measures
C. preventive measures
D. repressive measures

A. Incorrect. See section 5.6.5 of "*Foundations of IT Security*". Extinguishing a fire is a repressive measure. A stand-by arrangement is an example of a corrective measure, whereby fall-back means are put into service on an emergency basis in the event of a disaster. For example, using a different location in order to continue to work.

B. Incorrect. See section 5.6.3 of "*Foundations of IT Security*", Detective measures only give a signal after detection. When the direct consequences of an incident are not too large, or there is time to minimize the expected damage, detection can be an option. Ensure that each incident can be detected as soon as possible

C. Incorrect. See section 5.6.2 of "*Foundations of IT Security*", Prevention makes it impossible that the threat occurs. Examples in IT Security are: Disconnect Internet connections and internal network connections. Preventive measures are intended to avoid incidents.

D. Correct. Repressive measures, such as extinguishing a fire, are aimed at minimizing any damage that may be caused. Making a back-up is also an example of a repressive measure. See section 5.6.4 of "*Foundations of IT Security*".

See also section 5.9 of "*Foundations of IT Security*", Types of Risk Strategies.

11 of 40

What is an example of a human threat?
A. A USB-stick passes on a virus to the network.
B. Too much dust in the server room.
C. A leak causes a failure of electricity supply.

A. **Correct**. A USB-stick is always inserted by a person. Thus, if by doing so a virus enters the network, then it is a human threat. See section 5.7.1 of "*Foundations of IT Security*".
B. Incorrect. Dust is not a human threat.
C. Incorrect. A leak is not a human threat.

12 of 40

What is an example of a human threat?
A. a lightning strike
B. fire
C. phishing

A. Incorrect. A lightning strike is an example of a non-human threat.
B. Incorrect. Fire is an example of a non-human threat.
C. **Correct**. Phishing (luring users to false websites) is one form of a human threat. See section 5.7.1 and 10.6.2 of "*Foundations of IT Security*".

13 of 40

Information has a number of reliability aspects.
Reliability is constantly being threatened. Examples of threats are: a cable becomes loose, someone alters information by accident, data is used privately or is falsified.

Which of these examples is a threat to confidentiality?
A. a loose cable
B. accidental deletion of data
C. private use of data
D. falsifying data

A. Incorrect. A loose cable is a threat to the availability of information.
B. Incorrect. The unintended alteration of data is a threat to its integrity.
C. **Correct**. The use of data for private ends is a form of misuse and is a threat to confidentiality. See section 4.1.1. of *"Foundations of IT Security"*.
D. Incorrect. The falsification of data is a threat to its integrity.

14 of 40

A member of staff denies sending a particular message.
Which reliability aspect of information is in danger here?
A. availability
B. correctness
C. integrity
D. confidentiality

A. Incorrect. Overloading the infrastructure is an example of a threat to availability.
B. Incorrect. Correctness is not a reliability aspect. It is a characteristic of integrity.
C. **Correct**. The denial of sending a message has to do with nonrepudiation, a threat to integrity. See section 4.1.2. of *"Foundations of IT Security"*.
D. Incorrect. Misuse and/or disclosure of data are threats to confidentiality.

15 of 40

In the incident cycle there are four successive steps.
What is the order of these steps?
A. Threat, Damage, Incident, Recovery
B. Threat, Incident, Damage, Recovery
C. Incident, Threat, Damage, Recovery
D. Incident, Recovery, Damage, Threat

A. Incorrect. The damage follows after the incident.
B. **Correct**. The order of steps in the incident cycle are: Threat, Incident, Damage, Recovery. See section 6.5.4 of *"Foundations of IT Security"*.
C. Incorrect. The incident follows the threat.
D. Incorrect. Recovery is the last step.

16 of 40

A fire breaks out in a branch office of a health insurance company. The personnel are transferred to neighboring branches to continue their work.
Where in the incident lifecycle are such stand-by arrangements found?
A. between threat and incident
B. between recovery and threat
C. between damage and recovery
D. between incident and damage

A. Incorrect. Carrying out a stand-by arrangement without there first being an incident is very expensive.
B. Incorrect. Recovery takes place after putting stand-by arrangement into operation.
C. Incorrect. Damage and recovery are actually limited by the stand-by arrangement.
D. **Correct**. A stand-by arrangement is a repressive measure that is initiated in order to limit the damage. See section 6.5.4 and 5.6.1 of "*Foundations of IT Security*".

17 of 40

How is the purpose of an information security policy best described?
A. Policy documents the analysis of risks and the search for countermeasures.
B. Policy provides direction and support to the management regarding information security.
C. Policy makes the security plan concrete by providing it with the necessary details.
D. Policy provides insight into threats and the possible consequences.

A. Incorrect. This is the purpose of risk analysis and risk management.
B. **Correct**. The security policy provides direction and support to the management regarding information security. See section 9.2 of "*Foundations of IT Security*".
C. Incorrect. The security plan makes the information security policy concrete. The plan includes which measures have been chosen, who is responsible for what, the guidelines for the implementation of measures, etc.
D. Incorrect. This is the purpose of a threat analysis.

18 of 40

The code of conduct for e-business is based on a number of principles.
Which of the following principles do **not** belong?
A. reliability
B. registration
C. confidentiality and privacy

A. Incorrect. Reliability forms one of the bases of the code of conduct.
B. **Correct**. The code of conduct is based on the principles of reliability, transparency, confidentiality and privacy. Registration does not belong here. See section 9.3 and 10.5 of "*Foundations of IT Security*".
C. Incorrect. The code of conduct is based on confidentiality and privacy among other things.

19 of 40

A worker from insurance company Euregio discovers that the expiration date of a policy has been changed without her knowledge. She is the only person authorized to do this. She reports this security incident to the Helpdesk. The Helpdesk worker records the following information regarding this incident:
- date and time
- description of the incident
- possible consequences of the incident

What important information about the incident is missing here?

A. the name of the person reporting the incident
B. the name of the software package
C. the PC number
D. a list of people who were informed about the incident

A. **Correct**. When reporting an incident, the name of the reporter must be recorded as a minimum. See section 6.5.1 of *"Foundations of IT Security"*.
B. Incorrect. This is additional information that may be added later.
C. Incorrect. This is additional information that may be added later.
D. Incorrect. This is additional information that may be added later.

20 of 40

A company experiences the following incidents:
1. A smoke alarm does not work.
2. The network is hacked into.
3. Someone pretends to be a member of staff.
4. A file on the computer cannot be converted into a PDF file.

Which of these incidents is **not** a security incident?
A. 1
B. 2
C. 3
D. 4

A. Incorrect. A defective smoke alarm is an incident that can threaten the availability of data.
B. Incorrect. Hacking is an incident that can threaten the availability, integrity and confidentiality of data.
C. Incorrect. Misuse of identity is an incident that can threaten the aspect availability, integrity and confidentiality of data.
D. **Correct**. A security incident is an incident that threatens the confidentiality, reliability or availability of data. This is not a threat to the availability, integrity and confidentiality of data. See section 6.5 of *"Foundations of IT Security"*.

21 of 40

Security measures can be grouped in various ways.
Which of the following is correct?
A.   physical, logical, preventive
B.   logical, repressive, preventive
C.   organizational, preventive, corrective, physical
D.   preventive, detective, repressive, corrective

A.   Incorrect. Organizational/logical/physical is grouped around domains, and preventive/detective/repressive/corrective is grouped around the moment where a measure can be carried out in the incident chain. Preventive does not belong here.
B.   Incorrect. Organizational/logical/physical is grouped around domain,s and preventive/detective/repressive/corrective is grouped around the moment where a measure can be carried out in the incident chain. Logical does not belong here..
C.   Incorrect. Organizational/logical/physical is grouped around domains, and preventive/detective/repressive/corrective is grouped around the moment where a measure can be carried out in the incident chain. Organizational/physical or preventive/corrective does not belong here.
D.   **Correct**.   Preventive/detective/repressive/corrective   is   one   appropriate   group,   as   is organizational/logical/physical. See section 5.3 of "*Foundations of IT Security*".

22 of 40

A smoke alarm is placed in a computer room.
Under which category of security measures does this fall?
A.   corrective
B.   detective
C.   organizational
D.   preventive

A.   Incorrect. A smoke alarm detects and then sends an alarm, but does not take any corrective action.
B.   **Correct**. A smoke alarm only has a signalling function; after the alarm is given, action is still required. See section 7.9.1 of "*Foundations of IT Security*".
C.   Incorrect. Only the measures that follow a smoke alarm signal are organizational; the placing of a smoke alarm is not organizational.
D.   Incorrect. A smoke alarm does not prevent fire and is therefore not a preventive measure.

23 of 40

The Information Security Officer (ISO) of insurance company Euregio wishes to have a list of security measures put together.
What does he first have to do before security measures can be selected?
A.   Set up monitoring.
B.   Carry out an evaluation.
C.   Formulate information security policy.
D.   Carry out a risk analysis.

A   Incorrect. Monitoring is a possible measure, one should start with a risk analysis.
B.   Incorrect. Evaluation happens after the list of measures is assembled.
C.   Incorrect. An information security policy is important, but is not necessary in order to select measures.
D.   **Correct**. Before security measures can be selected, Euregio must know their risks to determine which risks require a security measure. See section 5 of "*Foundations of IT Security*".

24 of 40

What is the purpose of classifying information?
A.   To determine what types of information may require different levels of protection.
B.   To allocate information to an owner.
C.   To reduce the risks of human error.
D.   To prevent unauthorized access to information.

A.   **Correct**. The purpose of classifying information is to maintain an adequate protection. See section 6.4 of "*Foundations of IT Security*".
B.   Incorrect. Allocating information to an owner is the means of classification and not the purpose. See section 6.4 of "*Foundations of IT Security*".
C.   Incorrect. Reducing the risks of human error is part of the security requirements of the staff.
D.   Incorrect. Preventing unauthorized access to information is part of access security.

25 of 40

Strong authentication is needed to access highly protected areas. In case of strong authentication the identity of a person is verified by using three factors.
Which factor is verified when we must enter a personal identification number (PIN)?
A.   something you are
B.   something you have
C.   something you know

A.   Incorrect. A PIN code is not an example of something that you are.
B.   Incorrect. A PIN code is not something that you have.
C.   **Correct**. A PIN code is something that you know. See section 7.5 of "*Foundations of IT Security*".

26 of 40

Access to the computer room is closed off using a pass reader. Only the System Management department has a pass.
What type of security measure is this?
A.   a corrective security measure
B.   a physical security measure
C.   a logical security measure
D.   a repressive security measure

A. Incorrect. A corrective security measure is a recovery measure.
B. **Correct**. This is a physical security measure. See section 7 of "*Foundations of IT Security*".
C. Incorrect. A logical security measure controls the access to software and information, not the physical access to rooms.
D. Incorrect. A repressive security measure is intended to minimize the consequences of a disruption.

27 of 40

Four (4) staff members of the IT department share one (1) pass for the computer room. What risk does this lead to?
A. If the power fails, the computers go off.
B. If fire breaks out the fire extinguishers can not be used.
C. If something disappears from the computer room it will not be clear who is responsible.
D. Unauthorized persons may gain access to the computer room without being seen.

A. Incorrect. Computers going off as a result of a power failure has nothing to do with access management.
B. Incorrect. Even with one pass, the IT staff can put out a fire with a fire extinguisher.
C. **Correct**. Though it would be clear that someone from the IT department had been inside, it would not be certain who. See section 7.5.1 of "*Foundations of IT Security*".
D. Incorrect. No one has access to the computer room without a pass.

28 of 40

In the reception hall of an administration office, there is a printer which all staff can use in case of emergency. The arrangement is that the printouts are to be collected immediately so that they cannot be taken away by a visitor.
What other risk for the company information does this situation have?
A. Files can remain in the memory of the printer.
B. Visitors would be able to copy and print out confidential information from the network.
C. The printer can become defective through excessive use, so that it is no longer available for use.

A. **Correct**. If files remain in the memory they can be printed off and taken away by any passerby. See section 10.12.2 of "*Foundations of IT Security*".
B. Incorrect. It is not possible to use a printer to copy information from the network.
C. Incorrect. The unavailability of a printer does not form a risk for company information.

29 of 40

Which of the following security measures is a technical measure?
1. Allocating information to an owner
2. Encryption of files
3. Creating a policy defining what is and is not allowed in e-mail
4. Storing system management passwords in a safe

A. 1
B. 2
C. 3
D. 4

A. Incorrect. Allocating information to an owner is classification, which is an organizational measure.
B. **Correct**. This is a technical measure which prevents unauthorized persons from reading the information. See section 10.12.1 of *"Foundations of IT Security"*.
C. Incorrect. This is an organizational measure, a code of conduct that is written in the employment contract.
D. Incorrect. This is an organizational measure.

30 of 40

The back-ups of the central server are kept locked in the same enclosed room as the server. What risk does the organization face?
A. If the server crashes, it will take a long time before the server is again operational.
B. In the event of fire it is impossible to get the system back to its former state.
C. No one is responsible for the back-ups.
D. Unauthorized persons have easy access to the back-ups.

A. Incorrect. On the contrary, this would help to make the system operational more quickly.
B. **Correct**. The chance that the back-ups may also be destroyed in a fire is very great. See section 7.6.2 of *"Foundations of IT Security"*.
C. Incorrect. The responsibility has nothing to do with the storage location.
D. Incorrect. The computer room is locked.

31 of 40

Which of the following technologies is malicious?
A. encryption
B. hash
C. Virtual Private Network (VPN)
D. viruses, worms and spyware

A: Incorrect, encryption makes information unreadable to anyone except those possessing special knowledge, usually referred to as a key. See section 4.1.2 of *""Foundations of IT Security"*.
B: Incorrect, a hash function is a one-way encryption function that can be used to assure that data isn't changed. See section 8.6.4 *"Foundations of IT Security"*.
C: Incorrect: Depending on the configuration VPNs can be used to protect integrity and confidentiality of data when being transmitted. See section 10.9 of *"Foundations of IT Security"*.
D: **Correct**; These are all forms of malware, which establishes itself unrequested on a computer for malicious purposes. See section 10.6 of *"Foundations of IT Security"*.

32 of 40

Which measure does **not** help against malicious software?
A. an active patch policy
B. an anti-spyware program
C. a spam filter
D. a password

A. Incorrect. Malware often makes use of programming faults in popular software. Patches repair security leaks in the software, thereby reducing the chance of infection by malware. See section 5.1.1 of *"Foundations of IT Security"*.
B. Incorrect. Spyware is a malicious program that collects confidential information on the computer and then distributes it. An anti-spyware program can detect this malicious software on the computer. See section 10.7.6 of *"The Foundations of IT Security"*.
C. Incorrect. Spam is unrequested e-mail. It is often simple advertising but can also have malicious software attached or a hyperlink to a web site with malicious software. A spam filter removes spam. See section 10.6.3 of *"Foundations of IT Security"*.
D. **Correct**. A password is a means of authentication. It does not block any malicious software. See section 5.1.5 of *"Foundations of IT Security"*.

33 of 40

What is an example of an organizational measure?
A. back-up of data
B. encryption
C. segregation of duties
D. keeping network equipment and junction boxes in a locked room

A. Incorrect. Backing up data is a technical measure.
B. Incorrect. Encryption of data is a technical measure.
C. **Correct**. Segregation of duties is an organizational measure. The initiation, execution and control duties are allocated to different people. For example, the transfer of a large amount of money is prepared by a clerk, the financial director carries out the payment and an accountant audits the transaction. See section 4.1.2 of *"The Foundation of IT Security"*.
D. Incorrect. Locking rooms is a physical security measure.

34 of 40

Identification is establishing whether someone's identity is correct.
Is this statement correct?
A. yes
B. no

A. Incorrect. Identification is the process of making an identity known.
B. **Correct**. Establishing whether someone's identity is correct is called authentication. See section 8.3.5 of *"The Foundation of IT Security"*.

35 of 40

Why is it necessary to keep a disaster recovery plan up to date and to test it regularly?
A. In order always to have access to recent backups that are located outside the office.
B. In order to be able to cope with daily occurring faults.
C. Because otherwise, in the event of a far-reaching disruption, the measures taken and the incident procedures planned may not be adequate or may be outdated.
D. Because this is required by the Personal Data Protection Act.

A. Incorrect. This is one of the technical measures taken to recover a system.
B. Incorrect. For normal disruptions the measures usually taken and the incident procedures are sufficient.
C. **Correct**. A far-reaching disruption requires an up-to-date and tested plan. See section 9.4.1 of "*The Foundation of IT Security*".
D. Incorrect. The Personal Data Protection Act involves the privacy of personal data.

36 of 40

What is authorization?
A. The determination of a person's identity.
B. The registration of actions carried out.
C. The verification of a person's identity.
D. The granting of specific rights, such as selective access to a person.

A. Incorrect. The determination of a person's identity is called identification.
B. Incorrect. The registration of actions carried out is called logging.
C. Incorrect. The verification of a person's identity is called authentication.
D. **Correct**. The granting of specific rights, such as selective access to a person is called authorization. See section 8.3 of "*The Foundation of IT Security*".

37 of 40

Which important statutory norm in the area of information security do government bodies have to comply to?
A. Dependency & Vulnerability analysis
B. ISO/IEC 20000
C. ISO/IEC 27002
D. National information security legislation or regulations

A. Incorrect. Dependency & Vulnerability analysis is a risk analysis method.
B. Incorrect. ISO/IEC 20000 is a standard for organizing IT Service Management and is not compulsory.
C. Incorrect. ISO/IEC 27002 is the Code for Information Security. It is a guideline for organizing Information Security and is not compulsory.
D. **Correct**. National information security legislation or regulations are intended for all national governments and are obligatory. See section 11.2 of "*The Foundation of IT Security*".

38 of 40

On the basis of which legislation can someone request to inspect the data that has been registered about him or her?
A. Legislation regarding public records
B. Legislation regarding the protection of personal data
C. Legislation regarding computer criminality
D. Legislation regarding governmental information

A. Incorrect. Legislation regarding Public Records regulates the storage and destruction of archive documents.
B. **Correct.** The right to inspection is, in general, part of the legislation regarding the protection of personal data. See section 11.6 of "*The Foundation of IT Security*".
C. Incorrect. Legislation regarding computer criminality is aimed at making it possible to deal with offences perpetrated through advanced information technology. An example of such an offence is computer hacking.
D. Incorrect. Legislation regarding government Information regulates the inspection of governmental documents. Personal data is not a governmental document.

39 of 40

The Code for Information Security (ISO/IEC 27002) is a description of a risk analysis method. Is this statement correct?
A. yes
B. no

A. Incorrect. The ISO/IEC 27002 is a collection of controls based on best practices.
B. **Correct.** The ISO/IEC 27002 can be used in a risk analysis but is not a risk analysis methodology. See section 9.2.6 of "*The Foundation of IT Security*".

40 of 40

The Code for Information Security (ISO/IEC 27002) only applies to large companies. Is this statement correct?
A. yes
B. no

A. Incorrect. The Code for Information Security is applicable to all types of organizations, large and small.
B. **Correct.** The Code for Information Security is applicable to all types of organizations, large and small. See section 9.2 of "*The Foundation of IT Security*".

Appendix C   About the authors

The authors are all members of the Dutch Platform for Information Security and aim to make the field of information security more accessible for both information security specialists and departmental staff who are just starting out.

Hans Baars, CISSP, CISM, worked as information security officer and internal EDP Auditor at the police from 1999 to 2002. In 2002 he became consultant of integral security at the Dutch National Police Services Agency. In this position he was involved in formulating the information security policy of the Dutch police force. From 2006 he was working as a security consultant, during which time he advised government and commercial businesses on how to design their physical and information security. Since 2009 he is Chief Information Security Officer at Enexis BV, a Gas and Powergrid company in the Netherlands.

Kees Hintzbergen is account manager at 3-Angle. Kees has more than 20 years' experience in IT and information provision and has worked in the field of information security since 1999. In his everyday life Kees is a consultant, coach and 'mirror' where he employs the Common Sense Method. Thanks to his experience and his integrity, he is able to sell with his advice.

Jule Hintzbergen, CISSP PSP, after working initially for 21 years for the Ministry of Defense, has worked since 1999 at Capgemini as a public security consultant. Jule has more than 20 years' experience in IT and spends much of his time dealing with information security. He worked in various capacities in the area of project management, information management, physical and information security and biometrics. Since 2003 Jule has been certified CISSP at ISC2 and since 2007 is a certified PSP (Physical Security Professional) at ASIS International.

André Smulders (CISSP) is a senior information security consultant at TNO Information and Communication Technology. When André completed his Technology Management studies at the Technical University of Eindhoven in 1996, he started to work in the field of innovation and IT, and since 2000 he has specialized in information security. In his current role as consultant and programme manager he has been involved in information security projects varying from a technological level to a strategic level.

Index